# Conservation Heroes

# JOHN JAMES AUDUBON

# Conservation Heroes

Ansel Adams
John James Audubon
Rachel Carson
Jacques Cousteau
Jane Goodall
Al Gore
Steve and Bindi Irwin
Chico Mendes
John Muir
Theodore Roosevelt

# Conservation Heroes

# JOHN JAMES AUDUBON

Patrice Sherman

CHELSEA HOUSE
*An Infobase Learning Company*

**John James Audubon**
Copyright ©2011 by Infobase Learning

Chelsea House
An imprint of Infobase Learning
132 West 31st Street
New York, NY 10001

**Library of Congress Cataloging-in-Publication Data**
Sherman, Patrice.
  John James Audubon / Patrice Sherman.
    p. cm. — (Conservation heroes)
  Includes bibliographical references and index.
  ISBN 978-1-60413-953-2 (hardcover)
  1. Audubon, John James, 1785-1851—Juvenile literature. 2. Ornithologists—
United States—Biography—Juvenile literature. 3. Animal painters—United
States—Biography—Juvenile literature. I. Title. II. Series.
  QL31.A9S54 2010
  508.092—dc22
                    [B]    2010026480

Chelsea House books are available at special discounts when purchased in bulk
quantities for businesses, associations, institutions, or sales promotions. Please call
our Special Sales Department in New York at (212) 967-8800 or (800) 322-8755.

You can find Chelsea House on the World Wide Web
at http://www.chelseahouse.com.

Text design and composition by Annie O'Donnell
Cover design by Takeshi Takahashi
Cover printed by Bang Printing, Brainerd, MN
Book printed and bound by Bang Printing, Brainerd, MN
Date printed: January 2011
Printed in the United States of America

10 9 8 7 6 5 4 3 2 1

This book is printed on acid-free paper.

All links and Web addresses were checked and verified to be correct at the time
of publication. Because of the dynamic nature of the Web, some addresses and
links may have changed since publication and may no longer be valid.

# Contents

# John and Lucy: A Naturalist Meets His Match

The young man ushered into Lucy Bakewell's parlor that winter morning in 1804 must have looked very strange to her. Instead of wearing the sober browns and grays favored by the men of Montgomery County, Pennsylvania, he sported a brilliantly colored silk jacket and satin breeches. Rather than tie his long hair back into a neat ponytail, he let it hang loose over his shoulders in flowing chestnut-brown curls.

When he introduced himself as John James LaForest Audubon and asked if her father was home, she could hear his strong French accent. Yet he also said "thee" and "thou" like a Quaker, which was especially puzzling. Lucy's family belonged to the Unitarian Church, but she was friendly with her Quaker neighbors. She knew by his flamboyant appearance that Audubon certainly did not belong to the Society of Friends.

If his clothes and manners surprised her, however, she hid it well. At 16, she was quite mature for her age. She merely told him her father was out and would return in a few minutes. Meanwhile, Audubon was welcome to wait.

John James Audubon was born in Haiti, but spent his early years in France, until he moved to America at age 18.

The 19-year-old Audubon was perfectly happy to watch Lucy at her spinning wheel. Tall and slender, with smooth dark hair and large grey eyes, she mesmerized her visitor. "There I sat," he later wrote. "My gaze riveted, as it were, on the young girl before me who, half-talking, half-working, essayed to make the time pleasant for me."

In many ways, they were complete opposites. Lucy was reserved, while Audubon was outgoing. He acted on impulse. She made decisions slowly and deliberately. Yet as they talked, they discovered that they had much in common. Both were newcomers to the United States. Lucy had recently arrived with her family from England. Audubon had come alone from his home in Couëron, France, a year earlier. Both were gifted musicians: Lucy excelled at the piano, and Audubon played the flute and violin. They were avid readers, too. One of Lucy's favorite books was biologist Erasmus Darwin's *The Botanic Garden*. That must have pleased Audubon. *The Botanic Garden* had been a bestseller in Europe and he was no doubt familiar with the author's long poem on flowers and sexual reproduction, "The Loves of Plants."

What's more, Lucy had actually met Erasmus Darwin as a child. He was a close friend of her father. Darwin had encouraged William Bakewell to educate Lucy in the same manner as her brothers, with lessons in natural history and philosophy in addition to the traditional feminine tasks of cooking and sewing. As a result, Lucy loved outdoor life—another passion she and Audubon shared. Like him, she could hike for miles, ride horseback, and even swim, a remarkable accomplishment for a young woman at that time.

## "MY HEART FOLLOWED EVERY ONE OF HER STEPS"

When Lucy's father finally returned home he was not exactly pleased to find his oldest daughter deeply engaged in conversation with Audubon. Bakewell had already encountered Audubon several times out hunting and fishing in his fancy silk clothes. He knew the young man had been sent to Pennsylvania to help manage Mill Grove, an estate owned by his father, Captain Jean Audubon of France. The estate's overseer had discovered a lead mine on the property. Lead ore was a valuable resource and the mine was therefore a very profitable enterprise.

Audubon, however, had shown little interest in mining or any other productive labor. He had been seen at parties dancing, playing his fiddle, and flirting with girls. When he wasn't hunting or partying, he liked to roam through the woods, sometimes carrying a drawing pad and pens.

Bakewell didn't dislike Audubon. His sons had gone hunting with him and praised the Frenchman's marksmanship. Yet Lucy was nearly 17, a marriageable age. Bakewell hoped she would settle down with a prosperous gentleman farmer, not a 19-year-old artist-fiddler—no matter how good a rifleman he happened to be.

Perhaps to get Lucy out of the parlor and put an end to the budding romance, Bakewell asked her to go to the kitchen and prepare lunch. His ploy didn't work. "She now arose from her seat," Audubon recalled. "And her form, to which I had but paid partial attention, showed both grace and beauty. And my heart followed every one of her steps." He stayed for lunch.

Lucy's younger siblings, Thomas, William Jr., Sarah, Eliza, and Ann joined them. Audubon gallantly invited the entire family to dine at his home, a room he rented in a nearby farmhouse.

A few days later, Lucy must have felt as if she had entered Aladdin's cave. Audubon had transformed his entire living space into a treasure trove of natural history. Hollowed-out birds' eggs of every color and size dangled from the ceiling on long ribbons. Snake skins, turtle shells, preserved lizards, frogs, fossils, and dozens of other specimens crowded the shelves. The mantelpiece

## ERASMUS DARWIN (1731–1802): THE GRANDFATHER OF EVOLUTION

Most people know about Charles Darwin and his theory of evolution, but how many are aware that Darwin himself "evolved" from a family of scientists? His grandfather Erasmus Darwin was one of the most famous naturalists of the eighteenth century and introduced several of the ideas that led to the theory of evolution.

Born in 1731 in Nottingham, England, Erasmus Darwin studied medicine at Edinburgh University. Between 1783 and 1785, he published the first English translations of the works of Carl Linnaeus on the classification of species. After that, he wrote two long poems on botany, "The Loves of Plants" and the "Economy of Vegetation," which he published in a single volume, *The Botanic Garden*, in 1791. Darwin's frank references to the male and female parts of flowers shocked some of his readers. Apparently, they found the words *stamen* and *pistil*s too graphic for genteel society! Nevertheless, *The Botanic Garden* went on to become a bestseller and a classic of early botany.

In 1796, he published *Zoonomia,* a further inquiry into how life may have changed and developed over time. Erasmus Darwin's theories appeared similar to those of Jean-Baptiste Lamarck (1744–1829), who believed that animals could inherit acquired characteristics. In other words, if a giraffe stretched its neck to reach high leaves, displayed an array of stuffed squirrels, raccoons, and opossums. Every spare piece of wall was covered with paintings, mostly of birds.

After dinner, Audubon and his guests met a group of young people from neighboring farms for a skating party on the frozen river. The men pushed the women across the ice in small sleighs. "Each

its offspring would inherit longer necks. This theory was later disproved, but Darwin's emphasis on the importance of sexual reproduction did help his grandson Charles Darwin develop his own theories years later.

In addition to his pioneering work in natural history, Erasmus Darwin also devoted himself to social reform, especially the education of women. He advocated the establishment of female academies where girls would

Erasmus Darwin, a scientist and grandfather of Charles Darwin, was also a widely-read poet.

have the opportunity to study physiology, biology, geology, foreign languages, philosophy, and even manufacturing and finance—a radical notion for his time.

Though history remembers Charles Darwin far more than his grandfather, Erasmus Darwin certainly earned a place in both the history of science and in the evolution of equal rights for women.

fair one," he wrote, "was propelled by an ardent skater." Of course, Audubon made sure Lucy's skater was none other than himself.

## COURTSHIP AMONG PEWEES AND PEOPLE

As the weather grew warmer, Audubon spent most of his time exploring the countryside. During one of his walks, he spied the nest of a *Sayornis phoebe,* or common pewee flycatcher, above the entrance of a cave. It was, he noted, empty, "yet clean, as if the absent owner intended to revisit it with the return of spring."

He wondered, did some species of migratory birds return to the exact same nesting place every year? The next day, he got his answer: "As I entered the cave, a rustling sound over my head attracted my attention, and on turning I saw two birds fly off and alight on a tree close by—the Pewees had arrived!"

Audubon visited the cave daily, always careful not to disturb the birds. He observed them hunting insects, lining their nest, and courting one another. He became entranced by what he called "the delicate manner of the male bird to please his mate." When the female laid her first egg, he declared that he was as thrilled as he would have been "had I met with a diamond of the same size."

The pewees became so accustomed to Audubon's presence they allowed him to handle their six nestlings. Very gently, he lifted each young bird, tied a silver thread loosely around its leg, and returned it to the nest.

Bird banding had been used to track falcons in Europe since the Middle Ages, but Audubon's notes on the pewees are thought to be the first record of the practice in the United States.

The pewees were too wonderful a secret to keep to himself. Audubon wanted to share them with the one person who he knew loved nature as much as he did. Soon Lucy was coming to meet him in the cave every day. They watched the birds, read out loud to one another, and inevitably confessed their own blossoming attraction.

The habits of the *Sayornis phoebe*, or common pewee flycatcher, helped spark Audubon's early interest in birds.

Lucy knew that respectable young ladies of her world did not spend hours alone with young men in caves. Courtship was supposed to occur at home where they could be chaperoned by mothers, fathers, uncles, and aunts. But Lucy was no ordinary young woman of 1804. As the eldest daughter, she had frequently assumed responsibility for the household when her mother was ill. She was used to making independent decisions. Her father had always allowed her to come and go as she pleased.

Yet this time was different. When Bakewell heard about his daughter's excursions to the cave, he took her into his study and forbid her from seeing Audubon. Lucy never told Audubon what

*(continues on page 16)*

# BIRD BANDING: KEEPING TRACK OF THE WORLD'S PASSERINES

In 1595, villagers on the Mediterranean island of Malta captured a falcon. They soon realized this was no ordinary bird, for it bore on its leg a silver bracelet with the seal of King Henry IV of France. Eventually the bird was returned to the royal palace in Paris. It had flown almost 900 miles (1,450 kilometers) from home in only a few days.

The practice of banding valuable hunting birds in case they were lost or stolen goes back to the Middle Ages. Marco Polo recalled seeing falcons banded by Chinese noblemen during his travels through Asia between 1270 and 1295.

Several centuries later, the German ornithologist Johann Leonhard Frisch realized bands could be used to keep track of migratory birds, or passerines, as they were called. In 1740, Frisch banded several swallows to see if they would return the next year. No record remains of his results, but Audubon may have been thinking of Frisch's work when he banded the pewees at Mill Grove.

Scientists did not attempt large-scale banding until 1902, when Paul Bartsch, a biologist employed by the Smithsonian Institution in Washington, D.C., banded 23 black-crowned night herons. He inscribed each aluminum bracelet with an identification number, the year of banding, and the words "Return to the Smithsonian Institution." The first band arrived at his office a few months later, sent by a hunter who had shot one of the herons 55 miles (88 km) away in Virginia. Bartsch published the results of his banding experiment in 1904.

By 1909 there were so many bird-banding projects in North America that Leon Cole, a zoologist at the University of Wisconsin, formed the Bird Banding Association to enable people to pool their results. The U.S. Biological Survey Program took

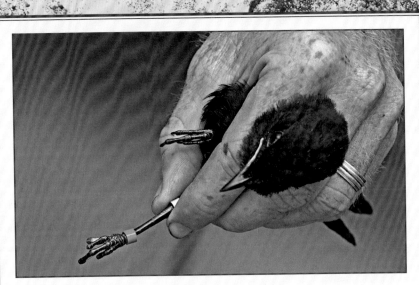

A Seychelles magpie robin, living on the Seychelles in the Indian Ocean, is banded so researchers can monitor the endangered species' population.

over the association in 1920, making bird banding a government enterprise.

The national program included amateur bird watchers as well as wildlife professionals. One of the most dedicated volunteers was Edward McIlhenny, a retired banker on Avery Island, Louisiana. From 1912 to 1942, he maintained a one-man bird-banding station where he banded 272,848 migratory waterfowl. Bands recovered from McIlhenny's birds revealed migration routes stretching from South America to the Arctic Ocean.

As of 2002, nearly every known species of bird throughout the world had been banded. In the United States alone, at least 85,000 bird bands are recovered each year. This information can be used to monitor endangered populations and help biologists ensure that even the rarest of birds will continue to return home, year after year.

*(continued from page 13)*

happened between her and her father that day. She must have made her case very eloquently, though, for Bakewell relented. Reassured that she and Audubon were doing nothing wrong, he gave Lucy permission to continue her unusual rendezvous, much to her delight.

That didn't mean Bakewell saw Audubon as an acceptable son-in-law. In late summer, he sent Lucy to her aunt and uncle in New York for a month, assuming the separation would bring the relationship to an end. He would have been very surprised, therefore, if someone had told him that Audubon would be spending the winter in bed under his very roof with Lucy right by his side.

A superb athlete, Audubon took special pride in his skating ability. One evening, he and Lucy's brothers were returning home from a hunting expedition, skating along the Pirkiomen River, their haul of grouse, wild turkeys, beavers, and squirrels draped over their shoulders. A dense mist had settled over slick, black ice. Audubon raced ahead to show off his speed. A moment later, he skated right into a hole. The powerful current seized him, sweeping him along under the surface. Just when his breath was about to give out, Audubon miraculously popped up in another hole. His friends saw him and rushed to drag him from the water.

At first, Audubon treated the escapade as a joke. A month later he started shaking with fever. The doctor told him he was suffering from an "abscess" (most likely pneumonia) and ordered him to stay in bed.

By that time Lucy had returned. She insisted Audubon be moved to the Bakewell home. He recuperated lying in the parlor. She devoted herself to him, nursing him until he was able to sit up, preparing his meals, reading aloud to him, and playing her piano for him each evening.

The Bakewell family was also in the midst of mourning. Lucy's mother had died that fall. Mrs. Bakewell had been ill a long time and her death was not unexpected. Still, it left Lucy with the conviction that she did not want to lose another person she loved. She would not give up Audubon. Her father, softened by his own grief, finally relented and consented to their marriage.

## HOPE SETS SAIL

While Audubon was busy courting Lucy, his father, Captain Jean Audubon, had become ensnared in financial difficulties. He had sold half of his Mill Grove estate and taken out a large loan, or mortgage, on the value of the other half to fund the lead mine. Unfortunately, the mine never made money. In addition, many of Captain Audubon's investments in France had failed.

Despite his dashing and aristocratic airs, Audubon was not the son of a rich man. His father was understandably reluctant to see him saddled with the responsibility of a family before he had a steady income.

To marry without parental consent would have been unthinkable for members of Lucy and Audubon's social class. Audubon needed a strategy. Ever optimistic, he swiftly decided to start an import business with Francois Rozier, a friend and fellow Frenchman. In the early nineteenth century the United States had relatively few manufacturing industries. The growing nation still depended on Europe for countless products, from carpenter's tools to china tea sets.

As soon as Audubon felt well enough to travel, he and Rozier booked passage to France on a ship appropriately named *Hope*. Once in Europe, they would establish contacts and seek funding for their business. Audubon also believed his new enterprise would impress his father enough to win the much-needed blessing for his marriage.

The *Hope* left New Bedford, Massachusetts, on March 12, 1805. Three weeks later Audubon sailed down the Loire River towards his childhood home, the village of Couëron, which he had not seen in three years. Though Audubon's father and stepmother welcomed him warmly, they worried about his safety. He was 20, old enough to be conscripted into Napoleon's army. If he did not want to be recruited by force, they warned, he should stick close to home.

Having spent nearly the entire winter confined to bed, Audubon had no intention of remaining indoors. He had promised to bring back some drawings of French birds for Lucy and a Spanish mule of good breeding stock for her father. Within a few days he was wandering through his old woodland haunts. Luckily, he didn't run into any members of the local militia. He did have the good fortune to encounter a 35-year-old doctor, Charles-Marie d'Orbigny, who was out on a similar mission to draw wildlife. Whereas Audubon was largely self-taught, d'Orbigny had received formal training in art. He became a mentor to the younger man, showing Audubon how to render the proportions of his figures more accurately through the use of perspective and foreshortening. Audubon stayed in France for a year, steadily improving his artistic technique while Rozier improved their financial prospects.

Meanwhile, Lucy was dealing with challenges of her own. Her widowed father had remarried a woman with whom she did not get along. She wrote to Audubon constantly, telling him how impatient she was for him to return so they could begin their new life together. Finally, on April 12, 1806, Audubon boarded a ship for the United States. He had one last misadventure before reaching land. A few days out at sea, pirates waylaid the vessel. They ransacked the passengers' possessions, taking any money and valuables they could find. Fortunately, Audubon and Rozier had stashed their gold in an old sock and escaped without loss.

Audubon called the pirates' ship the *Rattlesnake* and its sailors venomous predators. The *Rattlesnake,* however, could not poison his hopes. After disembarking in New York on May 27, he headed straight to Mill Grove, Pennsylvania, with his portfolio of new pictures and a fine Spanish mule. He was now free to do the two things he wanted most in the world: marry Lucy Bakewell and draw the birds of America. He knew he could not achieve the second without accomplishing the first.

# A Child of Revolution: Growing up in Haiti and France

On April 26, 1785, Jeanne Rabin, a 25-year-old Frenchwoman, gave birth to a son in the port city of Les Cayes, Haiti. She named him Jean after his father, Captain Jean Audubon. The two had met on board a ship bound from France to the Caribbean colony of Saint Domingue, as Haiti was then known. Jeanne had been hired as a chambermaid to one of the island's wealthy families. Captain Audubon was on his way to take charge of a sugar plantation he had recently bought.

The child received his mother's last name, Rabin, because his parents were not married. Captain Audubon already had a wife back home in France. Under most circumstances, the children of poor unwed mothers at that time could expect little help from their fathers. Perhaps because his own marriage had proved childless, though, Captain Audubon was pleased to have a son. He decided to raise young Jean in his own home with all the advantages of a legitimate child. The little boy spent his first years surrounded by luxury, waited on by slaves in the enormous plantation house and playing in the lush gardens that surrounded it.

Jeanne Rabin died when her son was two years old, shortly after giving birth to his sister, Rose. Her son grew up with only a vague memory of her face. Far more vivid were his recollections of pet monkeys, wild lizards, frogs, turtles, fish, and spectacular tropical birds. From the time he could walk he preferred to be outdoors. Birds fascinated him. "I felt an intimacy with them," he recalled in an essay about his childhood many years later. "None but aerial companions suited my fancy."

After a while, he no longer felt satisfied with simply watching birds. He wanted to possess them completely. Like most eighteenth-century boys, he had become familiar with hunting at an early age. Killing wild birds for sport and mounting them as decorations was a popular hobby among the upper classes. Stuffed birds only disappointed Jean. He could own them, but they appeared nothing like what they had been while alive. "The moment a bird was dead, however beautiful it had been in life, the pleasure arising from the possession of it became blunted," he lamented.

His father solved the problem by giving him a book about birds. When he saw the pictures, Jean had a revelation. Once captured on paper with pen and ink, a bird would be his forever. Though he didn't find the book's illustrations very realistic, the idea that he could paint birds filled him with purpose. "I turned over the leaves with avidity," he recalled. "[It] gave me a desire to copy nature." Barely six years old, Jean began drawing birds.

## A QUESTION OF FREEDOM

Captain Audubon believed strongly in freedom. During the American Revolutionary War he fought on the side of the colonists as a member of France's navy. He even witnessed the surrender of British General Cornwallis to George Washington in 1781. His ship, the *Queen Charlotte*, docked in Philadelphia after the war and he remained there for a few months, becoming acquainted with the

Pennsylvania countryside. Politically, he also supported the French Revolution of 1789, which removed King Louis XVI from the throne and turned France into Europe's first republic.

His sympathy with rebels, however, did not extend to slaves who sought freedom only a few miles from his own plantation. Most of Haiti's population consisted of African-Caribbean slaves. Europeans may have held all the power, but they formed only a small minority of the island's residents. The same year the French overthrew their monarch, Haitian slaves, supported by Africans who called themselves "free people of color," began to organize for equal rights.

Fearing the uprising would turn violent, many Europeans sold their property and fled. Captain Audubon, too, prepared to return home. First, though, he made a short trip to the United States in 1790 to purchase a large tract of land in Mill Grove, Pennsylvania. Ironically, he left his son Jean and his daughter Rose in the care of his own slaves, whom he apparently trusted with the lives of his children. That trust was not betrayed.

Captain Audubon sailed directly from the United States to his home in Nantes, France. A year later, in 1791, he sent for his children. As a bloody civil war ripped across the island, Jean and Rose were safely put aboard a ship, the *Tancrède,* and sent to France under the care of Martin Gatreau, a friend of the Audubon family. Six-year-old Jean Rabin was about to acquire a new nationality, a new home, a new mother, and a new name.

Anne Moynet, Captain Audubon's wife, welcomed Jean and Rose with the warmth of a true mother. Jean rapidly became her favorite. She was pleased by his interest in art, and when she discovered he also had musical skill, she hired a tutor to instruct him in the harpsichord and flute.

The Audubons lived in the village of Couëron, a few miles from the main city of Nantes. The forest there appeared every bit as inviting to Jean as the tropical gardens of Haiti. His parents enrolled him in the local school. If the weather was warm, however, he skipped class to spend the day exploring. When he returned with his backpack full of plants, insects, and feathers instead of lesson books, his stepmother refused to punish him. He could learn to read and write in his own way and time, she reasoned.

## TOUSSAINT LOUVERTURE: OPENING THE WAY FOR FREEDOM

The American Revolution was not the only war for independence in the New World. Between 1791 and 1803, the black residents of Haiti conducted the only successful slave rebellion in modern history. Their leader called himself *Louverture*, which literally means "the opening" and has sometimes been translated by some historians to mean "the one who opens the way."

Born in 1743 on Breda Plantation in La Cap, Haiti, Toussaint Louverture learned to read and write from his father, one of the few educated slaves in the region. When Louverture was 33, his master granted his freedom. He married and worked as a coachman to support his family, earning enough to rent a large plot of land. He even acquired slaves of his own, though he later freed them. Louverture also worked hard to further his own education. He read every dispatch from France he could get his hands on. News of the French Revolution filled him with hope. If all Frenchmen could be free, perhaps all Haitians could be, too.

The revolution did not immediately end slavery. In 1791, the new government declared that all black French subjects who were already free would be equal to whites. This did not prove to be a workable solution. The white planters considered it too much equality, and the blacks too little. Wealthy whites fled the island. Slaves, impatient for their freedom, rose in revolt.

Louverture quickly distinguished himself as a military leader. Under his command the rebels defeated the French forces in Haiti. In 1793, after two years of war, the French National Assembly

When he did go to school, he would usually come home with bruises from the fists of his fellow students. The other boys ridiculed Jean's Creole accent and ganged up on him. A few lessons

voted to end slavery. Louverture became Haiti's first black governor, a position he held for the next eight years.

In 1799, Napoleon seized power in France and reinstated slavery throughout the French colonies. Once more, Haitians rebelled. After another four years of war, Napoleon offered to grant Haiti independence on the condition that Louverture retire from politics once the treaty was negotiated. Louverture agreed.

The offer was a trap. As soon as he arrived at the negotiation site, French soldiers arrested Louverture and sent him to France. Napoleon imprisoned him

Toussaint Louverture led the first successful attempt by a slave population to overturn European colonialism.

without trial. Suffering from hunger and illness, Louverture died in jail on April 7, 1803. According to French records, he was buried in an unmarked grave.

The struggle in Haiti continued, culminating on November 18, 1803, with the Battle of Vertierres, which drove Napoleon's army from its last stronghold on the island. Haiti officially gained its independence on January 1, 1804. Though Louverture was not present at that moment, he is still recognized today as Haiti's greatest patriot and the father of his nation.

from a fencing master put a stop to the bullying. Jean was tall for his age and his walks in the woods had given him good physical endurance. His skill with a rapier in schoolyard contests won him a measure of respect, though he rarely challenged opponents.

Despite the fact that he was his father's biological son, Jean was not, according to French law, his father's legal heir. For the first few years he lived in France, he still went by the name Jean Rabin. In 1794, Captain Audubon and his wife completed the paperwork necessary for legal adoption. On March 7 of that year, a document signed in the Town Hall of Nantes declared him to be Jean Jacques Fougère Audubon. He was now officially Audubon, the name he would use for the rest of his life.

## THE TERROR

In 1793, the very type of murderous violence that caused Captain Audubon to flee Haiti spread across France in a bloody wave. Maximilien Robespierre, a man of high ambitions and deep suspicions, had taken control of the government in Paris. Those who were hailed as champions of the Revolution one day found themselves accused of treason the next. The guillotine sent thousands to their death. People called it the Reign of Terror.

On New Year's Day 1794, the Terror arrived in the city of Nantes. Under the command of Robespierre's agents, soldiers rounded up nearly 9,000 citizens deemed "enemies of the Revolution." Some were beheaded, some shot, and many taken out onto barges in the Loire River, tied together, and thrown into the river to drown.

Captain Audubon was among those arrested. It was not unusual for whole families to be imprisoned together, and it is possible that his wife and children were incarcerated with him, though the historical record is not clear on this point. It is fairly clear that young Audubon was aware of the slaughter in Nantes even if he did not witness it himself. As an adult, Audubon never spoke directly about the Terror. He did, however, comment that he found his own species to be far more savage than any kind of bird or animal he knew.

Fortunately, Captain Audubon had influential friends on the city council. He was released unharmed within a few months. After that, the family stayed in Couëron and rarely ventured into the city. Audubon, now nearly 10, retreated to the silence of the forest and the company of his beloved birds.

## THE END OF THE REVOLUTION

In 1799, a young general named Napoleon Bonaparte seized power in France. The revolution was effectively over. Monarchy, with Napoleon as emperor, had returned to the nation. People began to enjoy some degree of social stability and prosperity once more.

In Nantes, Audubon's parents realized the time had come to find a career for their 14-year-old son. At first, they assumed he would follow in his father's footsteps into the navy. Two years earlier, in 1797, Audubon had served a brief stint as a cabin boy on a vessel used to train naval officers. At first, he had enjoyed the new adventure. Among his many other natural gifts, Audubon was ambidextrous, meaning he could use both hands equally well. This gave him a tremendous advantage in tying knots and clambering up the ship's rigging. He learned to swim and loved the sensation of being in the water. His skill with the flute and violin, coupled with his artistic ability, made him popular among the other boys, enabling him to make friends for the first time in his life.

Unfortunately, he also suffered from severe seasickness. What was worse, he had no taste for military discipline. He failed to pass the final exam for admission to the officer's school. Much to his parents' disappointment, he returned home. Once there, he happily went back to wandering in the woods, seeking out birds to observe and draw.

## JOHN JAMES AUDUBON OF AMERICA

By his late teens, Audubon was frankly a mystery to his parents. Though obviously bright and talented, he was no more interested in pursuing a university degree than he had been in joining the

(*continues on page 28*)

# NAPOLEON:
# THE GOLDEN EAGLE OF FRANCE

Although Audubon did not want to join Napoleon's army, he admired the general and considered him a role model. Both men were outsiders in France; Audubon came from Haiti and Napoleon from the Mediterranean island of Corsica. Both had endured teasing at school because of their foreign accents. Both had started their careers in obscurity, Audubon as a wandering artist and Napoleon as a second lieutenant in the French artillery.

Indeed, Napoleon's rise to power inspired Audubon when he decided to seek a wider audience for his own work. "Since Napoleon became, from the ranks, an Emperor," he wrote in 1826, "why should not Audubon be able to leave the woods of America a while and publish and sell a book? . . . I will try, by heaven until each and every hair about me will have dropped from my body, dead and grey with old age!!"

Napoleon, it seemed, evoked strong emotions from everyone on both sides of the Atlantic. Some condemned him as a brutal conqueror. Others praised him as a brilliant leader.

He acquired his first taste for politics during the French Revolution when he took control of a complicated battle in Corsica among the royalists, revolutionaries, and Corsican natives. His success in bringing the island under French control impressed the new government and gained him a promotion to Lieutenant Colonel.

Though he was briefly arrested in 1793 during the Reign of Terror, Napoleon had a knack for being able to remain on the right side of whichever faction was in power. When Italy invaded France in 1797, his swift victory over the enemy made him a popular hero at home. The following year, in 1798, he led French troops on an invasion of Egypt. He brought with him a group of scientists to collect Egyptian artifacts and study the natural environment. Among them was the physicist Jean Fourier, whose observations on heat later laid the foundation for the theory of the greenhouse effect in the twentieth century.

Upon returning to France in 1799, Napoleon found the government in chaos. Seeing his opportunity, he enlisted the help of a small group of loyal supporters and staged a takeover. On November 9, 1799, Napoleon became the dictator of France. Weary of

Napoleon's actions shaped European politics in the 1800s.

civil unrest, the people welcomed his rule. Five years later, on December 2, 1804, he had himself crowned emperor of France at Notre Dame Cathedral in Paris. He took as his symbol the golden eagle of the old Roman Empire and called himself the Eagle of France.

As emperor, Napoleon introduced the metric system, established a centralized department for higher education, and strengthened government support for the French Academy of Sciences. His military ambitions, however, eventually led to his downfall. After losing to the British at the Battle of Waterloo on July 15, 1815, he was exiled to the island of St. Helena, where he died in 1821. He remains one of history's most controversial figures to this day.

*(continued from page 25)*

navy. The question of what to do with him became especially critical in 1802, when Napoleon began drafting young men into the army by force.

The property that Captain Audubon had purchased in Pennsylvania provided a solution to their dilemma. The overseer whom Captain Audubon had hired to manage Mill Grove sent a letter telling him that lead had been discovered on the property. The captain saw this as the perfect opportunity for his son to escape the draft and hopefully acquire practical experience in farming and business management.

In August 1803, 18-year-old Audubon boarded a ship for the United States. Before he departed, his father told him three things: First, he should learn English as soon as he could. Second, he should apply for U.S. citizenship when he turned 21. Third, his name, in keeping with his new American life, would now be John James LaForest Audubon.

# Becoming
# an American

When Audubon first arrived in the United States he was delirious—not with joy, but with yellow fever. The disease had swept up the east coast from Philadelphia to New York, leaving thousands dead. After his ship docked on the East River, Audubon disembarked briefly to change his French francs into U.S. dollars at a bank in Greenwich Village. He returned to the ship shaking and dizzy. The ship's captain, John Smith, immediately recognized the symptoms of the disease. Smith was a personal friend of Audubon's father. Rather than deposit the young man in a New York hospital, which was little more than a pest house, he took a few days off from his duties to escort Audubon to a boarding house in Norristown, Pennsylvania, that was run by two Quaker women.

Audubon's caretakers had nursed many patients through the fever. He had not been stricken too seriously and after a few weeks the danger passed. While he recovered he learned English, copying the Quakers' use of the pronouns *thee* and *thou* in place of *you*. This is what so startled Lucy Bakewell when she met him a few months later.

Over the years Lucy must have become accustomed to it, for Audubon continued to address her with *thee* and *thou* throughout their entire marriage. Even after he learned regular English, the old-fashioned terms remained his way of expressing his affection for the woman he called his "dearest friend" and "matching soul."

A few months after his twenty-first birthday, Audubon took his father's advice and applied for U.S. citizenship at the Pennsylvania District Court in Philadelphia on September 5, 1806. He used his new Americanized name, John James Audubon. Due to a backlog of government paperwork, he would not officially become a citizen until 1812, but he always considered 1806 to be the true date of his naturalization.

## DUCK HUNTING IN MANHATTAN

For two years, between 1806 and 1808, Audubon and his business partner Francois Rozier lived in New York and worked for Lucy's uncle Benjamin Bakewell, the manager of an import-export company. Lucy's father had set up the employment in order to give them a little experience before they launched their own business.

Rozier was sincerely interested in becoming a merchant. Audubon had little enthusiasm for working behind a counter, but he valiantly did his part. "I am always in Mr. Bakewell's store where I work as much as I can," he wrote Lucy a few months after arriving. The minute he was free, however, he took off for the woods.

In the early nineteenth century, New York City occupied only the lower part of Manhattan. The upper part of the island still consisted of wilderness—a wilderness filled with birds. During 1807, Audubon drew 27 species of ducks, including the canvas back, pintail, and common merganser.

Audubon had no objection to eating his specimens after he was through drawing them. In fact, his journal often included notes on the bird's flavor as well as its appearance. He and Rozier were short on funds, so Audubon's hunting did double duty, providing both food for his art and nourishment for his body.

At this time Audubon also realized he needed to learn more about taxidermy if he wanted to recreate the life-like poses he preferred for his drawings. A friend introduced him to Dr. Samuel Latham Mitchell, a taxidermist and professor of natural history at Columbia University. Mitchell hired Audubon as his part-time assistant to help him stuff and mount a variety of animals for his natural history collection.

Audubon quickly discovered there was definitely something "fishy" about this job. Rumors had circulated through New York that doctors were robbing graves in order to dissect dead bodies. One night, neighbors complained to the authorities about an alarming smell coming from Dr. Mitchell's house. Local constables banged on the door, demanding entrance. Instead of

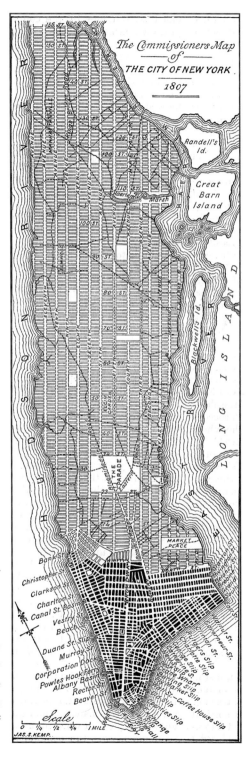

**This 1807 plan of Manhattan Island (part of New York City) shows that the bottom tip of the city was more developed than the wilderness and marshes of the northern end.**

This 1812 image of New York City's Harlem neighborhood—now filled with paved streets lined with buildings—was once a vast plain filled with grass and trees.

finding a cut-up corpse inside, they saw Audubon stuffing an embalmed fish.

When he wasn't working on taxidermy, Audubon took advantage of Mitchell's large library, where he could read the latest scientific treatises from Europe, among them Erasmus Darwin's *Zoonomia: Or the Laws of Organic Life.*

## A NEW FRONTIER

Audubon and Rozier decided that Louisville, Kentucky, was the best location to open their fledgling general store. They weren't the only young men of their generation to head west. In 1803, President Thomas Jefferson had purchased a vast territory from France that stretched from the Mississippi River to the Rocky Mountains. Encompassing 828,800 square miles (2,146,500

# LEWIS AND CLARK: AMERICA'S CORPS OF DISCOVERY

On November 18, 1803, Meriwether Lewis and William Clark, accompanied by a troop of 33 men, started their expedition across North America to the Pacific Coast. No white man had ever undertaken this journey before. President Thomas Jefferson, who had commissioned the expedition, called them the Corps of Discovery.

Jefferson charged the corps with three tasks: first, to map the geography of the territory they passed through; second, to make contact with the native tribes there; and third, to collect and describe any plants and wildlife they found. Jefferson himself studied natural history and thought Lewis and Clark might actually discover woolly mammoths living on the other side of the Mississippi River.

During the late eighteenth century, the bones of an ancient elephant-like creature had been unearthed in Big Bone Lick, Kentucky. Before departing on his journey, Lewis had visited the site and spoken to Dr. William Godforth, the excavator. Though the French zoologist Georges Cuvier had introduced the idea of extinction in 1796, scientists were not yet convinced that some fossils came from species that no longer existed. Many believed living specimens might still be found in unexplored regions of the globe.

Lewis and Clark, of course, did not encounter any mammoths. They did find at least 178 different plants, as well as 122 species and subspecies of animals—22 of which had never been seen by Europeans. These included the grizzly bear, pronghorn deer, black-tailed prairie dog, white-tailed jack rabbit, and western rattlesnake.

The explorers identified eight new species of birds, among them a large red-breasted woodpecker they called *Melanerpes lewis,* or Lewis's woodpecker, and *Nucifraga columbiana,* or Clark's nutcracker, a small gray and white bird that dwells in pine forests. They

*(continues)*

*(continued)*

also came across flocks of enormous swans, some with a wingspan of nearly 7 feet (2 meters). The loud, nasal cry of those birds suggested the name trumpeter swan (*Cygnus buccinators*). Averaging 60 inches (153 centimeters) high from feet to beak and weighing about 28 pounds (12.7 kilograms), the trumpeter is the largest swan in the world. In 1836, 30 years after Lewis and Clark's expedition, Audubon painted a life-size portrait of a young trumpeter swan for the final folio of *Birds of America*.

Clark's Nutcracker, named after explorer William Clark, can be found in western North America from British Columbia and western Alberta in the Canadian north to Baja California and western New Mexico in the south.

Lewis and Clark returned from the Pacific, ending their journey at St. Louis, Missouri, on September 23, 1806. They brought back treasures ranging from dried lichens to a necklace of grizzly bear claws made by one of the tribes along the Missouri River. Their most valuable gift to the nation, however, was their many notebooks and journals. Housed today mainly at the American Philosophical Society in Philadelphia, these volumes are now available online for everyone who wants to read about one of the boldest expeditions ever undertaken and one of the greatest adventures ever told.

square kilometers), the Louisiana Purchase doubled the size of the United States.

Between 1804 and 1806, the explorers Meriwether Lewis and William Clark traversed this territory and the western lands beyond it. They returned with stories of fantastic animals, plants, and birds. Audubon had certainly heard of Lewis and Clark. He knew establishing a business in Kentucky was not only practical, but it would also open his eyes to a whole new natural world.

On April 5, 1808, Audubon and Lucy Bakewell wed in a small ceremony attended by her family and a few mutual friends. Afterward they packed up their few belongings and set off for America's new frontier.

Louisville was the gateway to that frontier. Settlers speaking English, German, and Dutch stopped off on their way down the Mississippi River to the Southern bayou, or up the Missouri to the western plains. French trappers and Native Americans came into town to trade animal pelts for manufactured goods. African Americans lived there, too. Most were slaves, though the black community also included free people.

The Audubons easily made a place for themselves in this vibrant, but sometimes violent society. Tall and athletic, Audubon impressed everyone with his excellent horsemanship, his steady aim with a rifle, and his courage in the face of danger. When a pair of river pirates threatened to make off with a settler's livestock, Audubon jumped into the fight. Calling upon the fencing lessons he had learned back in France, he beat the thieves off wielding only a long pole in place of a sword.

Lucy was far less flamboyant, but her intelligence, education, and gentle manners soon won her a circle of admiring female friends. The couple rented rooms in a boarding house called the Indian Queen, where they dined at long tables with everyone from traveling preachers to roaming rum dealers. If this was not the type of companionship Lucy was used to, she never complained. Her only regret, she wrote to a cousin in England, was that she had not brought more books with her, "for there is no library here

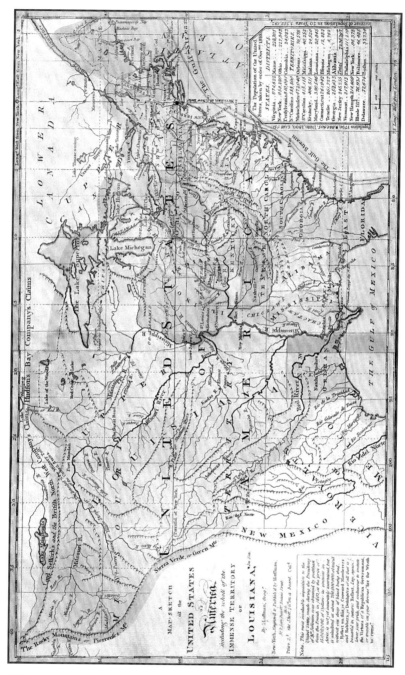

This map of the United States, created circa 1812, shows the "whole of the immense territory of Louisiana." It also notes population figures from the 1810 census.

or bookstore of any kind, and as Mr. Audubon is constantly at the store, I should very much enjoy a book while I am alone."

## A KENTUCKY BARBECUE

It was a slight exaggeration for Lucy to tell her cousin that Audubon was constantly at the store he and Rozier had recently opened in Louisville. Nor was Lucy herself alone. What the town lacked in literary resources, it more than made up in outdoor activities. Both Audubon and Lucy swam together in the river every morning when the weather was warm, and also rode horseback. Dances and picnics filled the summer months.

Everyone looked forward to the Fourth of July, for the people of Louisville celebrated all day and far into the night with music, contradancing, horse races, target practice, barbecue, and "flagons of every beverage used in the country," including plenty of home-brewed whisky.

Twenty years later, Audubon would recall Independence Day as the high point of his life in Louisville. "The whole neighborhood joined with one consent. No personal invitation was required where everyone was welcomed by his neighbor," he wrote in his essay "Kentucky Barbeque [sic] on the Fourth of July." They assembled in a beech woods on the banks of Beargrass Creek. The women wore long, white dresses and the men fringed hunting shirts and deerskin trousers. When an orchestra of "violins, clarinets, and bugles gave the welcome notice," more than a hundred couples formed two lines, facing one another for the cotillion dance. Partners joined hands and whirled around, the fringe on the men's shirts keeping time, Audubon noted, with the swaying of the ladies' ruffled skirts.

The dancers dined on barbecued ham, venison, turkey, beef, and fish, followed by a dessert of peaches, plums, melons, and pears. "In a word," he concluded, "Kentucky, the land of abundance, had supplied a feast for her children." A feast, indeed, that he never forgot.

## TWO AMERICAN ORNITHOLOGISTS

Audubon's favorite place for hunting birds around Louisville was at the Ohio River Falls, a series of rapids at the edge of the city's port. Amid the rocky ledges he found kingfishers, indigo buntings, and scarlet tanagers.

Audubon's fascination with birds sometimes made his neighbors doubt his sanity. The sight or sound of a bird could cause him to drop everything and take off in hot pursuit. On one occasion he abandoned his horse, laden with a large packet of money from the store, to chase a wild bird through the forest. Someone found the horse

### ALEXANDER WILSON: AMERICA'S FIRST ORNITHOLOGIST

Alexander Wilson's background was, if anything, even more unusual than Audubon's own story. Born in 1766 to the son of a whisky distiller in Paisley, Scotland, he was apprenticed to a weaver at the age of 13. His real passion, however, was writing poetry. His poems were mainly criticisms of the factory owners who were driving the old-fashioned weavers out of business. His opinions caused so much trouble that he was forced to flee to America to avoid arrest.

In 1794, Wilson settled near Philadelphia, not far from Mill Grove, where Audubon was to reside nine years later. Though he had little more than a grammar school education, he took up school teaching. The famous American naturalist William Bartram became his friend and mentor. Bartram, who had written several books on native plants and animals, suggested Wilson start a series of books on American birds.

It is not clear if Wilson had any previous interest in ornithology or art, but he must have warmed to his subject very readily. In 1804, at the age of 40, he started traveling throughout the eastern rambling riderless along the road and returned both horse and money to Lucy, so no harm was done. Nevertheless, Audubon must have thought no one in all of America could possibly be as obsessed by birds as he was. He felt so different from other men who only hunted for food or pleasure. He sought knowledge, though he couldn't yet say what he intended to do with that knowledge.

All that changed in 1810, when a middle-aged Scotsman in a shabby overcoat and worn boots wandered into Audubon's store and laid two enormous books upon the counter. His name was Alexander Wilson and he had recently rowed his way from Pittsburgh

United States in search of birds to draw. The first leg of his journey took him north to Niagara Falls, where he wrote "The Foresters," a 2,200-line epic poem describing the people and wildlife he found there.

During the next 10 years, Wilson traveled more than 10,000 miles (16,100 km), mostly on foot or in a rowboat. By the time he arrived at Audubon's store in 1808, he had published two volumes of his nine-volume series called *American Ornithology*.

The completed work depicted more than 260 species of birds, including 48 Wilson had discovered himself. Several of these species bear his name, among them Wilson's storm petrel, Wilson's plover, and Wilson's warbler. French ornithologist Charles Lucien Bonaparte later named an entire genus of warblers *Wilsonia* in his honor.

Though Wilson is not as well known as Audubon, historians still consider him America's first major ornithologist. The University of Michigan established the Wilson Ornithological Society in 1886, the same year that George Bird Grinnell founded the Audubon Society in New York. In 2006, the *Wilson Bulletin* became the *Wilson Journal of Ornithology*, one of the few scientific journals devoted entirely to the study of birds.

to Louisville in a boat he called the *Ornithologist*. He said he had heard Audubon was interested in birds, and so he had something to show him. When he opened the books, Audubon saw they were filled with drawings of birds.

Wilson told Audubon he was selling subscriptions to a series of books he called *American Ornithology*. When Audubon later told the story of their encounter, he claimed he was initially interested in buying a subscription to Wilson's work, but Rozier objected. Why would Audubon want to buy someone else's drawings of birds, Rozier asked, when his own pictures were so much better?

Until he saw Wilson's books, Audubon had given little thought to his long-term goals. The idea of creating a book had never occurred to him. Great scholars like Erasmus Darwin wrote books, not frontier storekeepers like Audubon.

Now Wilson's visit had made him see his work in a new light. If this man, who had no more formal education then he did, could write a book on birds, why couldn't he write one, too? Gradually, a new idea formed in Audubon's mind. He would write a book on the birds of America and it would be bigger, better, and more beautiful than any other.

# Seeking a Wilder Range

L ife in Louisville may have been pleasant for Audubon, but it was not profitable. Competition among merchants in the fast-growing city proved fierce, and their store had not done as well as Audubon and his partner Rozier had hoped. In the spring of 1810, Rozier suggested they move their business to Henderson, Kentucky, a new frontier town 125 miles (200 km) down the Ohio River from Louisville. Henderson was the jumping-off point for settlers headed west to the juncture of the Ohio and Mississippi rivers. A general store would offer travelers a good place to stock up on provisions for the long journey.

Audubon agreed to the plan. He had thoroughly explored the forests around Louisville and seen all the birds there. "I longed to find a wilder range," he later wrote in his journals. That June, he and Lucy piled all their belongings onto a large, flat-bottomed boat and paid a pair of river men to pole them down to their new home.

The trip was not easy for Lucy. A year earlier, on June 12, 1809, she had given birth to their first child, Victor Gifford Audubon. The little boy was as active and curious as his father. Keeping watch over him on a boat that lacked any railings must have been a challenge. Nevertheless, Victor's energy delighted both his parents. "A single smile from our infant," Audubon wrote, "was more valuable than all the treasures of a modern Croesus." Among all their possessions, he declared, "our child's cradle was our richest piece of furniture."

The Audubons received as warm a welcome in Henderson as they had in Louisville. The young family moved into an authentic log cabin and celebrated their arrival by sharing a feast of biscuits and bacon with their new neighbors.

Everything started out well. The log cabin served as the store until they could construct a separate building. Rozier took charge of the business operations, selling gunpowder, woolen cloth, axes, iron nails, salt, flour, and any other necessities he could supply. Audubon hunted and fished to ensure a good supply of meat. Lucy cooked, cleaned, cared for Victor, planted a garden, and gathered wild fruits, including blackberries, elderberries, grapes, beech plums, crab apples, and paw-paws, a fruit that tasted like custard when ripe.

Audubon didn't have the patience to stand for hours with a rod and reel in his hand, so he learned to fish by setting out a "trot line." This was a long, single line spanning the river like a clothesline, from which he dropped shorter lines into the water baited with frogs and weighted with stones. The catfish of the Ohio River grew to legendary proportions, reaching 25 pounds (11 kilograms) or more. In the true frontier tradition of tall tales, Audubon bragged that he once caught a big catfish and discovered a whole perch in its stomach when he cut it open. A friend then replied that he had caught one that had swallowed a suckling pig.

Western Kentucky was a land of big fish, big game, and big birds. In July 1810, Audubon saw his first ivory-billed woodpecker. The largest of the North American woodpeckers, the ivory-bill had a wingspan of nearly 3 feet (1 m). According to one story, an early frontiersman who saw the bird had exclaimed, "Lord God, what a

Years after he first saw an ivory-billed woodpecker, Audubon included an image of the bird in his large-format 1827 to 1838 folio book *Birds of America*.

bird!" Ever since then, the ivory-bill was known as the Lord God Bird. Audubon called it "the great chieftain of the woodpecker tribe." He also remarked that travelers were willing to pay a quarter apiece for the brilliant red heads of the birds, which they wore as

## THE IVORY-BILLED WOODPECKER: GHOST OR SURVIVOR?

In April 1999, David Kulivan, a forestry student at Louisiana State University, spied two unusual birds while out duck hunting on Pearl River in southeastern Louisiana. The birds clung to the trunk of a tree like woodpeckers, but they were far larger than any Kulivan had seen before. In addition, each bird had a triangular white patch on its back and white edging on its wings. Kulivan estimated that he observed the birds for at least 10 minutes. Though he had a camera, he did not use it because he was afraid any movement might disturb them. When he returned to the university, he described the birds to several ornithology professors. When he finished, they told him he had seen a living ghost.

The last confirmed sighting of an ivory-billed woodpecker had taken place in 1944. Despite rumors that the bird still existed in remote areas, the International Union for the Conservation of Nature officially declared the ivory-bill extinct in 1994.

News that two ivory-bills had been seen in Louisiana set off a frenzy of activity among ornithologists. Over the next decade, expeditions from Cornell University, Auburn University, and the University of Windsor in Ontario combed the Gulf Coast from Louisiana to the Florida panhandle, searching for any trace of an ivory-billed woodpecker.

Because the ivory-bill prefers to stay beneath the dense forest canopy, it is difficult to get a clear view of the bird in flight ornaments. Audubon did not object to this practice, but he did note that ivory-bills were hard to find. Hunters had to follow them for miles through some of the most "oozy, mirey, spongy" swampland he'd ever seen.

when its distinctive markings are most visible. In 2006, a wildlife preservation group called Corridor of Hope offered a $10,000 reward for any information leading the U.S. Fish and Wildlife Service to an ivory-bill nest or feeding site in the state of Arkansas. The Cornell Lab of Ornithology upped the ante by promising $50,000 to the first person to lead a biologist to a living ivory-billed woodpecker.

The ornithologists received hundreds of tips. In 2006, 2007, and 2008, searchers took videos of birds they believed to be ivory-bills. None of the images was clear enough to provide definitive proof. Skeptics derided the search as a "wild woodpecker chase," as foolish as the proverbial wild goose chase. The big bird's elusiveness even inspired cartoonists, who depicted it as a sly Woody Woodpecker character peeking out from behind the trees at frustrated bird watchers.

Cornell University called off its search in 2009. That same year, the team from Auburn and the University of Windsor announced they would continue to accept information, but would no longer update their Web site. In 2010, ornithologist Ron Rohrbaugh, leader of Cornell's original search team, told the press, "We don't believe a recoverable population of ivory-billed woodpeckers exists."

Not everyone, however, is ready to give up. Some biologists believe efforts should focus on preserving the ivory-bill's habitat rather than trying to find the bird itself. There is still hope, they insist, that one day someone will look up, see an enormous woodpecker with white-tipped wings fly by, and exclaim, "Lord God, what a bird!

During the summer of 1810, Audubon drew the ivory-billed woodpecker, the scarlet tanager, white pelicans, and sandhill cranes. He also began to write his captions on the pictures in English rather than French, indicating that he was finally becoming as American on the page as he felt in person.

Business success, however, still eluded Audubon and Rozier. As winter closed in, the partners decided they would try selling their goods at the trading post of Ste. Genevieve, slightly more than 100 miles (160 km) north of Henderson on the Mississippi River. This time Lucy stayed behind, moving in with neighbors who would help her while her husband was gone. In return, she promised to tutor their children in reading and writing.

Assured that his family would be safe, Audubon set off with high hopes for bird hunting. The forests of the Upper Mississippi were even less settled than those around the small village of Henderson. Now, at last, he would find the "wilder range" he longed for.

## AMONG THE SHAWNEE

Audubon and Rozier departed a few days before Christmas in the middle of a snowstorm. Their keelboat, Audubon estimated, traveled about 5 miles (8 km) per hour with the current. On the third day they offered a ride to a French count and his father-in-law who were on their way to Ste. Genevieve. When the four men reached the entrance to the Mississippi, they discovered the river had iced over. They turned back and docked their boat on the shores of Cache Creek, French for "hidden creek," in what is now southern Illinois.

They found about 50 Shawnee families already camped along the shore. Audubon had learned a few words of Shawnee in Henderson and many of the Shawnee knew some French from their dealings with trappers. A lively conversation ensued, during which Audubon managed to convey his interest in local wildlife. The Shawnee responded by bringing him the pelts of small animals, horns, bones, teeth, and other "curiosities of natural history" in exchange for knives and a pair of scissors. Unlike most Europeans, Audubon did not refer to Native Americans as "savages." To the contrary, he wrote about his admiration for their culture, noting that the Shawnee women expressed their gratitude for the scissors "as gracefully as the most educated female would have done."

Rozier took no interest in the Shawnee. He and the count's father-in-law huddled morosely on the boat, bored and angry, while Audubon and the count, who was an expert huntsman, mingled with the Shawnee. The Frenchmen argued among themselves. Audubon despised Rozier's hostile attitude. They could not go anywhere until

Audubon was very interested in the Shawnee's culture and knowledge of wildlife and enthusiastic about the chance to briefly live and hunt with them. This photo shows a reconstruction of a Shawnee village.

the ice melted, he pointed out, so why not take advantage of the opportunity to learn as much as possible from their hosts?

The next morning Audubon awoke and saw a group of Shawnee men and women boarding canoes for a hunting expedition. He hastily dressed and asked permission to join them. A moment later, he had seated himself in the bottom of a canoe that was "well supplied with ammunition and whiskey."

The hunting party crossed the river to the feeding ground of an enormous flock of wild trumpeter swans. After securing the canoes, the women headed into the woods to gather pecans. The men began the swan hunt. First, three scouts deliberately startled the birds, causing them to fly upwards. As the birds took wing, the Shawnee took aim. Within a few minutes, Audubon counted at least 50 dead birds floating feet up and head down in the water. He knew the Shawnee were not just hunting for food. The swans' skins would be swapped at Ste. Genevieve for knives and guns. The feathers would eventually end up on the hats of wealthy Englishwomen.

There is no evidence in Audubon's journals that he condemned this trade. He killed birds himself occasionally, simply to draw them. He never blamed the Shawnee for the slaughter of the swans. And yet, his references to the "beautiful birds . . . struggling in the last agonies of life" just to adorn the hats of fashionable ladies suggests that his sympathy lay with the swans, not with the Ste. Genevieve merchants who profited from selling their feathers abroad.

A few days after the swan hunt, three young Shawnee men invited Audubon on a bear hunt. The party tracked a bear to its cave about a mile from the camp. The Shawnee leading the group told Audubon to climb a sapling, which would keep him safe; a bear would not try to climb a tree that was too slender to hold its weight. Audubon readily obeyed. He had never hunted a bear before and had no desire to meet one in its lair. From his perch, he watched the leader enter the cave while the other two Shawnee waited at the entrance. After a few moments the leader emerged and told Audubon he could come back down. The bear was dead.

The bear was an essential source of food for the Shawnee tribe. In this case, Audubon did not mourn the animal's death. He considered the man who had faced the bear alone a "hero." Looking back many years later, he wrote, "I have seen many Indian exploits, which proved to me their heroism." Few white men of his generation thought of Native Americans as heroes.

## AMONG THE OSAGE

In early January, Audubon said his farewells to the Shawnee and set out again for the Mississippi River with his companions. They made their way part way up the river with help from a party of six trappers who offered to pilot their boat in return for provisions. Progress was slow. They had to abandon their oars, instead using towlines to pull the boat along the shore. Every morning, they rose two hours before dawn and pulled until dusk. The water was so thick with ice floes that they traveled less than 7 miles (11 km) a day. Audubon didn't mind the strenuous labor. While trudging along with the towline on his back, he wrote, "I kept my eyes on the forest or on the ground, looking for birds or curious shells."

The river froze solid again and they decided to wait out the cold weather in an area known as Tawapatee Bottom. The wilderness there elated Audubon. "What a place for winter quarters!" he wrote. "Not a white man's cabin within 20 miles (32.1 km) on the other side of the river, and on our own, none within at least 50 (80.4 km)!"

The men, now a party of 10, built a sturdy cabin in a matter of days. Audubon explored the surrounding woods, where he encountered a number of Osage and Shawnee hunters. He was eager to learn more about the Osage, but he did not know their language, and they spoke neither French nor English.

He did note that they were even better shots with the bow and arrow than the Shawnee, and preferred big game such as elks, bear, and buffalo to small animals or birds. Audubon described the Osage as "athletic" and "robust." They were good looking and tall: The men averaged 6 feet (183 centimeters), while most male Europeans at that time were only 5 feet 4 inches (162 cm). Earlier explorers had also remarked upon their habit of bathing twice a day in warm weather, quite shocking to the white men, who seldom

## FRANCIS LA FLESCHE: PRESERVING THE OSAGE LEGACY

The Osage considered their language, music, and rituals essential to their sense of national identity. By the early twentieth century, however, their traditions had begun to die out. Only a few older people spoke the native language or sang ritual music. Those voices, which formed the very last links to their earlier culture, might have been lost forever if it hadn't been for Francis La Flesche, Native American anthropologist, linguist, and scholar.

Born in 1857, La Flesche belonged to the Omaha Nation, a tribe closely related to the Osage. In his early twenties, he worked with Alice Cunningham Fletcher, an anthropologist who studied Native American tribes for the Smithsonian Institution. As Fletcher's assistant, La Flesche became an expert in operating the newly invented Edison cylinder recording machine. One of the first people he recorded was his own father, Joseph Iron Eye La Flesche, the last chief of the Omaha Nation selected by traditional rituals.

Around 1911, he began to record the rituals and ceremonies of the Osage. He was a meticulous researcher and worked tirelessly to track down any member of the tribe who knew authentic songs and chants. His goal was to obtain a complete version of every Osage ceremony. By 1929, he had made 254 separate recordings.

For decades La Flesche's recordings lay on shelves, almost forgotten. Cylinders had become an antique technology. No one had bathed at all. The Osages called the French "Heavy Eyebrows," and the English "Long Knives." They called themselves "Little Ones," not because they thought they were small, but out of respect for their gods.

the machines to play them anymore. Fortunately, the development of digital technology in the late twentieth century enabled historians to duplicate the recordings. When contemporary Osage people heard the voices of their great-grandparents and great-great-grandparents, they said they felt as if they had discovered the Dead Sea Scrolls of the Osage Nation.

La Flesche also started to compile a dictionary of the Osage language. He died in 1932 before completing the project. Today, the Osage continue his work through the Osage Nation Language Program, which offers classes to tribal members of all ages.

Francis La Flesche was the son of the last Omaha chief, Iron Eyes. La Flesche interpreted Omaha culture for western ethnologists visiting the reservation and did his own research on the music and rituals of the Osage.

According to Osage educators, the mission of the program is "to teach our people to speak Osage within the realm of our unique ways and in daily conversation." A living language, they say, is essential to a living culture: "Our future depends on it."

Unlike the Shawnee, the Osage did not like to mix with the Europeans, perhaps fearing their independence would be compromised. As a gesture of goodwill, Audubon visited their camp. Unable to communicate with language, he used art, drawing portraits of several young men with red chalk. The results apparently pleased the Osage, for Audubon wrote that "they laughed to excess" at his work.

Audubon and his party stayed at Tawapatee for six weeks. Hunting was excellent. The men hung so much meat from the trees, Audubon joked, that the forest around their cabin resembled a butcher's shop. Now that they had enough food, Audubon spent his days at camp drawing deer, cougar, raccoons, turkeys, and other wildlife. At night the men built a campfire, piling up 10-foot-long (3-m-long) logs until the structure towered at least 7 feet (2 m). Atop the logs, they placed dry brush and kindling. They lit the fire by striking a flint against steel. Within an hour, the fire would be so hot, Audubon declared, that it "would roast you at a distance of five paces."

The Osage took to dropping by the camp in the evening. The women would tan deer skins while Audubon and one of his companions played the flute and fiddle. Sometimes the European men would jump up and dance, a performance that never failed to send the women into gales of laughter. The Osage men, by contrast, merely stood on the edges of the campfire, smoking "tomahawk pipes" and regarding the festivities in silence.

One morning in early March, Audubon and his fellow travelers awoke to what they thought was a volley of gunshots. They soon realized the sound came from the river. They rushed down to the shore and found the ice breaking up with thunderous cracks. Ice floes, big as log cabins, went soaring into the air and plummeted back down, smashing everything in their path. The men heard something crash downstream. An ice dam had given way. Four hours later, the current surged by. The great Mississippi had begun to roll again.

Audubon and Rozier resumed their journey, reaching Ste. Genevieve in late March. They enjoyed some well-earned success there:

The whiskey they had obtained in Louisville for 25 cents a gallon (3.7 liters) sold for two dollars a gallon to the thirsty French trappers. Rozier, pleased to be among French-speaking people, thought they should settle in Ste. Genevieve permanently. Audubon, however, wanted to get back to Lucy. He considered himself an American now. He spoke and wrote in English, not French. Tensions between the two partners reached a breaking point. Rozier was tired of Audubon's need to wander off on his own in the woods. Audubon felt Rozier had no interest in anything outside of business. They settled matters by deciding to dissolve their partnership. Rozier would stay in Ste. Genevieve and open a store, while Audubon would return to Henderson and continue the business there alone.

Audubon did not want to hazard another trip via boat, so he chose to walk home, traveling the entire 165 miles (265 km) across Illinois to the Kentucky-Ohio border on foot. He made the trip in less than a week, completing about 45 miles (72 km) a day by walking from sunrise to sunset. The muddy ground slowed him down somewhat. On good terrain, Audubon could maintain a pace of 7 to 8 miles (11 to 13 km) an hour, faster than most people can run.

He arrived in Henderson on a clear evening in early April. Neighbors called out to greet him. Lucy, with Victor in her arms, ran to meet him. No matter how much Audubon had enjoyed his adventures in the wild, he was glad to be home.

# Audubon
# the Businessman

In the spring of 1811, just as Audubon was starting his trek from Ste. Genevieve to Henderson, a brilliant comet began to trace its way across the sky. At night it shone brighter than any celestial object except the moon. Throughout the world, people speculated upon what its appearance might mean. Since ancient days, comets had been considered omens of major changes. Though this may be only superstition, the Great Comet of 1811 certainly seemed to fit the bill.

In the United States, the summer of 1811 was the hottest on record. The woods became so dry that people lived in constant fear that a single spark could start a wildfire. The season ended with a complete solar eclipse on September 17, further spreading anxiety and doubt. When Robert Fulton's new steamboat the *New Orleans* arrived in Louisville on October 28, it sent so much smoke into the sky that onlookers fled in terror, convinced that the comet itself had fallen into the Ohio River and the end of the world had come.

# SIGNS AND SCIENCE:
# THE GREAT COMET OF 1811

For nearly nine months in 1811, people around the globe were able to see one of the brightest comets in recorded history traveling across the night sky. Contemporary astronomers believe it had an apparent magnitude of 0. That may not sound very bright, but "apparent magnitude" assigns the lowest numbers to the most visible objects in the sky and the highest to the dimmest. Most stars have an apparent magnitude of 4 to 5. The Great Comet, therefore, was about five to six times brighter than the average star. In addition, it had a spectacular tail, at times as long as 25°, meaning it stretched one quarter of the distance from the horizon to the summit of the sky.

French astronomer Honoré Flaugerues discovered the Great Comet on March 25, 1811, while observing Mars through a small telescope. By late summer the comet could easily be seen with the naked eye. In Oregon, Alexander Ross, a Canadian fur trader, wrote in his journal that on September 1, 1811, he "observed, for the first time, about 20 degrees above the horizon, and almost due west, a very brilliant comet, with a tail about 10 degrees long." The Native Americans of the Pacific Northwest called the comet *Skom-malt-squisses* and hailed it as a good omen. Europeans, too, considered the comet to be a sign, though not necessarily a positive one. In Western mythology, comets are frequently associated with war and disaster.

Winemakers, however, experienced an excellent year. Even today the appearance of a comet is thought to bring good weather and a successful grape harvest. There is no scientific evidence for this, but the label Comet Vintage is still used to indicate a superior bottle of wine.

*(continues)*

*(continued)*

This nineteenth century engraving shows people's startled reaction to the appearance of the Great Comet in 1811.

The Great Comet of 1811, now called C/1811 F1, remained visible for 260 days, a record broken only by the comet Hale-Bopp, whose visit lasted a total of 617 days from July 23, 1995 to April 1, 1997. When will the C/1811 F1 return? Its orbit has been calculated at 3,065 years, so Earth won't see the Great Comet of 1811 again until 4876.

Audubon and Lucy were visiting friends in the city at the time and witnessed these events. Audubon was far too rational to believe the apocalypse had come. He did note, however, that the steamboat was "the *n'est plus ultra* in transportation," meaning that there was no better way of traveling down the river.

The *New Orleans* was the first steam-driven vessel to travel from Pittsburgh all the way to New Orleans. Within a few years, dozens of steamers would be plying the Mississippi River, carrying merchants, farmers, craftsmen, traders, teachers, gamblers, and even artists like Audubon to every city along its banks.

Important changes were occurring among nations, too. Tensions between the United States and England had reached a crisis point, propelling both countries towards war. In Europe, Napoleon had expanded his empire across the continent and started pushing into Russia.

Yet in Audubon's world, none of that compared to the day the earth moved in New Madrid, Missouri. On December 16, 1811, the first of a series of three massive earthquakes rocked the lower half of the United States. The impact was felt as far north as Canada and as far west as the Rocky Mountains. At the epicenter, the shocks caused the Mississippi River to roll backwards, engulfing steamboats and causing hundreds of people to drown. In Boston, Massachusetts, 1,000 miles (1,600 km) away, ground tremors made church bells chime.

Audubon lived barely 100 miles (160 km) away in Henderson, Kentucky. The quake hit while he was out horseback riding. At first he thought the distant rumbling signaled an oncoming thunderstorm, and he tried to spur his horse home. The horse refused to move, bracing its four legs against the ground, hanging its head, and emitting loud groans. The next moment, Audubon saw the trees around him shake. Beneath him, the ground surged like an ocean wave. He clung to his horse, the two of them rocking together, he wrote, "like a child in a cradle." Much to Audubon's relief the quake stopped after a few minutes. His horse needed no encouragement to return home. As soon as the ground settled down, the horse "brought his feet to the natural position, raised his head and galloped off as if loose and frolicking without a rider."

The initial quake was followed by two more on January 23 and February 7, 1812. All three quakes are believed to have measured at least 8.1 on the Richter scale, making them among the fiercest to

In the aftermath of the New Madrid, Missouri earthquakes, destruction and flooding were devastating problems.

strike the continental United States. Severe aftershocks continued to plague the New Madrid area until March 15.

Once more, people thought the dire predictions inspired by the Great Comet had come true. The end of the world, at last, was here. Audubon, by contrast, became so accustomed to the shocks that by the time they declined, he claimed he positively enjoyed the sensation of the earth rocking beneath his feet!

## THE HAWK IN FLIGHT

If Audubon had been superstitious, he might have thought the comet brought him good luck. During the summer of 1812, he and Lucy took their son Victor to meet her family in Pennsylvania, their first visit in three years. Lucy's brother Tom Bakewell became Audubon's new business partner, replacing Rozier. Even better, the youngest of the Bakewell brothers, 12-year-old Will, became Audubon's eager assistant, scrambling up the tallest trees to locate bird nests.

When Will discovered a female broad-winged hawk brooding on her eggs, Audubon instructed him to cover the hawk with his handkerchief and bring it back down. Amazingly, Will succeeded. For the next couple of hours, the hawk perched quietly on a stick in Audubon's studio, flexing its wings while he sketched it. It even allowed him to touch it. Audubon confessed he felt "quite uneasy" when the bird looked at him with its "sorrowful" eye. After he finished his drawing, he carried the hawk to the window and it flew off "without uttering a single cry."

The completed drawing showed the hawk with one wing extended as if about to take flight. Few naturalists at that time attempted to depict birds in flight, relying instead on stiff, almost wooden poses. Audubon preferred his subjects to appear as dramatic and lifelike as possible, and the broad-winged hawk represented a significant breakthrough for him as an artist.

On July 3, 1812, Audubon took the U.S. oath of citizenship, one of the proudest moments of his life. Five months later, on November 30, the Audubons had yet another cause for celebration when Lucy gave birth to their second son, John Woodhouse Audubon. At the age of 27, Audubon felt good fortune had finally begun to come his way.

## TAKING CARE OF BUSINESS

For six years, from 1813 to 1819, Audubon and Thomas Bakewell worked hard to maintain a successful general store in Henderson, Kentucky. Audubon had less time for exploring the wilderness, but he didn't seem to regret it. He and Bakewell opened a second store in Shippingport, a settlement close to Louisville. They bought and sold real estate, and made plans to construct a steam-powered sawmill and gristmill for grinding grain into flour.

Audubon found himself regarded as a prosperous young businessman among Henderson's growing middle-class community. He built a new home for his family and furnished it in style. Lucy purchased a piano, four silver-backed mirrors, damask tablecloths, silver candlesticks, china dishes, cast iron pokers for the fireplace, finely crafted furniture of cherry wood, walnut, and maple, and enough pots and pans to equip her busy kitchen. Audubon acquired three new guns, powder horns, a new flute and fiddle, a map of the world, a silver compass, a microscope, a walnut desk, a library of more than 150 volumes, and a hunting dog named Juno.

He trained Juno to retrieve live birds, much to the delight of his two young sons. Juno brought them seven wild ducklings whose mother had been shot and the Audubons raised them as domestic fowl. They also rescued a wounded turkey, which Audubon named Tom; he ruled the henhouse until he returned to the wild. Audubon failed to recognize the turkey when he spotted it on the road one day, but Juno knew his old friend instantly and refused to chase it down.

Audubon never ceased to be fascinated by animal behavior. How did the dog recognize the turkey, he wondered. "Was it the result of instinct . . . or the act of an intelligent mind?" Many years later he wrote, "Every time I read or hear of a stupid animal in a wild state, I cannot help wishing that the stupid animal that speaks thus was half as wise as the brute he despises." In other words, the only "stupid animals," as far as he was concerned, were the people who underestimated the intelligence of their fellow creatures.

## THE PASSENGER PIGEON

Audubon used the time he spent traveling between the stores at Henderson and Shippingport to keep up his study of nature. In the autumn of 1813, he witnessed one of the most phenomenal displays of bird life in North America. Upon leaving his house, he noticed flocks of passenger pigeons flying overhead. After riding a few miles, he stopped and tried to count them by making a dot on a piece of paper for every flock. Within 21 minutes he had 163 dots. As he

Swarms of migratory passenger pigeons once blanketed some parts of the country, and they were popular birds to hunt for sport. The last remaining flock of these now-extinct birds was killed by hunters in 1896.

watched, a hawk began to chase the pigeons, forcing them into a single, dense cloud. He wrote:

> I cannot describe to you the extreme beauty of their aerial evolutions. At once, like a torrent and with a noise like thunder, they rushed into a compact mass, pressing upon one another in the center. In these almost solid masses, they darted forward in undulating and angular lines, descended and swept close over the earth with inconceivable velocity, mounted perpendicularly so as to resemble a vast column, and, when high, were seen wheeling and twisting within their continued lines, which then resembled the coils of a gigantic serpent.

Audubon illustrated male and female passenger pigeons in his book *Birds in America*. The image was engraved and colored in London. Audubon's original watercolor was purchased by the New York Historical Society, where it is still on display.

Historians have praised Audubon's essay on the passenger pigeon as his best piece of writing, and for good reason. In it, he demonstrates his ability to look at nature with both the eye of the artist and the curiosity of the scientist.

After rhapsodizing about the beauty of the flock, Audubon tried to calculate just how many birds there were. He estimated that the entire flock was about 1 mile (1.6 km) wide and traveled overhead at a rate of 1 mile per minute, with two pigeons per yard (meter) of aerial space. If the flock took three hours to pass, it would cover about 180 miles (290 km). If that was the case, the number of birds would therefore be 1,115,136,000.

He went on to calculate that, since the average passenger pigeon consumed one-half pint (2.75 deciliters) of food per day, the flock would devour 8,712,000 bushels (307,000 dl) of grain every 24 hours. (Audubon may have been using measurements that are slightly different from modern ones. Current U.S. volume measurements would make it about 7,486,805 bushels.)

The only mistake Audubon made in his calculations was that the flock he was watching did not take three hours to pass overhead. It took three days.

When the pigeons came down to roost in the forest, whole trees collapsed beneath their weight. Pigeon excrement lay several inches thick on the ground, "like a bed of snow," Audubon noted wryly.

As soon as the pigeons alighted, hundreds of men armed with guns, clubs, burning torches, spears, and any other weapons they could find moved in for the kill. All night, as more and more pigeons arrived, the men beat, burned, pierced, and shot nonstop. "It was a scene of uproar and confusion," Audubon wrote. Attracted by the smell of blood, wolves, cougars, raccoons, polecats, bears, eagles, and hawks descended for their share of the feast. Between the thunderous sound made by the pigeons' wings, the howls of the predators, and the gunshots, Audubon couldn't even hear the person standing next to him.

By dawn the hunters had gathered the pigeons into piles and started plucking and salting them on the spot. Those too mangled for human food were fed to hogs. Audubon concluded that although the slaughter looked terrible, it did not diminish the number of pigeons, for each pair of surviving birds produced between two and four offspring per year. He did add, with great foresight, that "nothing but the gradual diminishment of our forests can accomplish their decrease."

## THE LAST PASSENGER PIGEON

At one o'clock in the afternoon on September 1, 1914, Martha died at the age of 29 in the Cincinnati Zoo. Named for Martha Washington, Martha the passenger pigeon was the last of her species. After her body had been stuffed and mounted, it was exhibited at the Smithsonian Institution in Washington, D.C. The label on the glass case said: "Extinct."

Ornithologists estimate that there were between 3 billion and 5 billion passenger pigeons living in North America when Europeans began to settle the continent in the seventeenth century. About 25 percent, or 1 out of every 4 birds, was a passenger pigeon. The pigeon's habitat extended from Nova Scotia across southeastern Canada, through the midwestern United States and down to the Gulf Coast.

In the eighteenth and nineteenth centuries, passenger pigeons became the main source of meat for poor people and slaves. In 1805, Audubon noted that a whole bird could be bought in the markets of New York for a penny. The use of nets increased the number of birds that could be killed in a single season. By the 1850s,

Audubon, it turns out, was partially right. The last passenger pigeon died in 1914. The species had been driven to extinction as much by the destruction of its habitat as by hunting.

## THE GREAT FINANCIAL PANIC OF 1819

In 1819, yet another disaster struck the United States. Unlike an earthquake, it could not be immediately felt, but it proved just as

the passenger pigeon population had declined enough to cause concern among naturalists. In 1857, a group of ornithologists in Ohio introduced a bill to protect the passenger pigeon. They were laughed out of the state legislature.

Over the next 40 years, the destruction of forests to build railroads and cities hastened the pigeon's decline. Passenger pigeons were highly social birds and could only breed in large groups. They needed vast stretches of woodland to nest and could not reproduce in captivity. After hunters destroyed the last remaining flock at its nesting place in Petowsky, Michigan, in 1896, the passenger pigeon was doomed. A teenage boy killed the last wild pigeon in Pike County, Ohio, on March 24, 1900.

Several zoos maintained small numbers of pigeons in captivity. Among them was a pair named George and Martha at the Cincinnati Zoo. George died in 1909, leaving Martha the only passenger pigeon on the planet.

The extinction of the passenger pigeon served as a wake-up call to Americans. Within a decade of Martha's death, legislation had been enacted to protect endangered birds. A bronze statue of Martha now stands at the Passenger Pigeon Memorial, part of a national historic landmark at the Cincinnati Zoo.

devastating, if not more so. The first great economic depression in the United States drove thousands of businesses into bankruptcy, including that of Bakewell and Audubon.

The causes of the depression were complex. For many years, getting credit from banks had been easy: To help businesses get started, the government had encouraged banks to make loans and authorized the Department of the Treasury to print more money, setting the stage for inflation. At the same time, the government itself had to borrow money to finance the War of 1812, creating debts that came due when peace was declared in 1814. In addition, harsh weather conditions had caused crops to fail in 1816 and 1817, leaving farmers without any money to spend.

Without customers, businesses began to fail. Banks seized the property of those who could not pay back their loans. As cash became scarce, people panicked. All those who had lent money demanded payment, whether or not the debtors had the means to pay. Bakewell and Audubon had borrowed money from many different investors to finance their saw mill and grist mill. Now those investors wanted their money back, but the mills had just started operating and had yet to show a profit.

In 1816, Audubon and Bakewell had sold a small steamboat they owned for a promissory note of $4,250. The buyer had promised to pay within a year. When he failed to deliver the money in 1817, Audubon went down to New Orleans to retrieve the boat, hoping they could sell it to someone else. He learned it was at the bottom of the river. Audubon exchanged harsh words with the buyer, Samuel Bowen, who insisted the boat had been damaged at the time of purchase. Audubon called Bowen a thief. Bowen retorted that Audubon was a cheat.

Audubon returned to Henderson with Bowen following right behind him. The two men came to blows one morning in the middle of the street. Audubon had to fight one-handed, for his right arm was in a sling due to an injury he had suffered in the mill. Despite his disadvantage, he displayed remarkable coolness. Bowen started the fight, hitting Audubon 12 times with a club. Audubon endured the blows silently. He made no effort to defend himself until Bowen's shouts had attracted a crowd of witnesses. Then he stabbed Bowen with his left hand, inflicting a serious wound.

In court, the witnesses swore Audubon had acted in self-defense. A judge cleared him of all charges, stating, "Mr. Audubon, you have committed a grave offense—an exceedingly serious offense—in failing to kill the damned rascal."

## DARK DAYS

Unfortunately, Audubon's street fighting skills could not help him fight the banks. Unable to pay his debts, he declared bankruptcy. He and Lucy sold everything they owned at an auction, including his crayons, pencils, paints, drawing paper, the seven wild ducks they had raised from infancy, and the cherry wood cradle they had once called their most cherished possession. The sale of their entire household netted about $25,000, the equivalent of more than $350,000 in 2010 currency. That still did not cover their debts.

Having sold his horse, Audubon walked 200 miles (320 km) to Louisville seeking work. Instead of a job, he found his creditors waiting for him with a warrant for his arrest. He was thrown into jail. Once again, the law was on his side. The financial panic had landed so many people in debtor's prison that the state of Kentucky had decided to abolish the institution. The judge freed Audubon a few days later.

Audubon returned home embittered by the whole experience. Only Lucy saved him from despair. "She gave me the spirit such as I really needed," he wrote in his journal. Lucy arranged for them to move in with her sister and brother-in-law, Eliza and Nicholas Berthaud, in Louisville.

The family set off for Louisville with nothing but the clothes on their backs. Lucy, who had recently given birth, carried their infant daughter, Rose, in her arms. Audubon carried a loaf of bread and a sack of apples. Nine-year-old Victor Gifford and seven-year-old John Woodhouse trudged alongside their parents. They ate their meager supper sitting by the banks of the Ohio River. Years later, when his sons were grown men, Audubon would write them a letter describing his feelings at that moment: "At that day, the world was with me as a blank . . . My heart was sorely heavy, for scarcely had I enough to keep my loved ones."

Yet that was also the great turning point in his life. "Through those dark days," he told his sons, "I was being led to develop the talents I loved." Even without his pencils and paints, Audubon was still an artist and his art would save them.

# Audubon the Artist

John James Audubon did not like to accept charity outright. In exchange for the Bertrauds' hospitality, he offered to draw Nicholas Bertraud's portrait. Ironically, the Bertrauds had been the major buyers of Audubon's household goods. Now they kindly returned his drawing materials to him.

Bertraud was so pleased with the portrait that he recommended Audubon to others. Within a few months, Audubon had a steady stream of clients paying him as much as five dollars for a single pencil and charcoal portrait.

Before the invention of photography, a hand-drawn picture was the only image families could have of a departed loved one. Portrait artists were often called upon at all hours of the day or night to sketch people as they lay dying. Parents, especially, wanted to preserve the memory of a child. One grieving couple even had their recently buried son removed from his grave just so Audubon could draw a portrait. Drawing the dead boy must have haunted Audubon. He and Lucy had lost an infant daughter themselves in 1815. Their

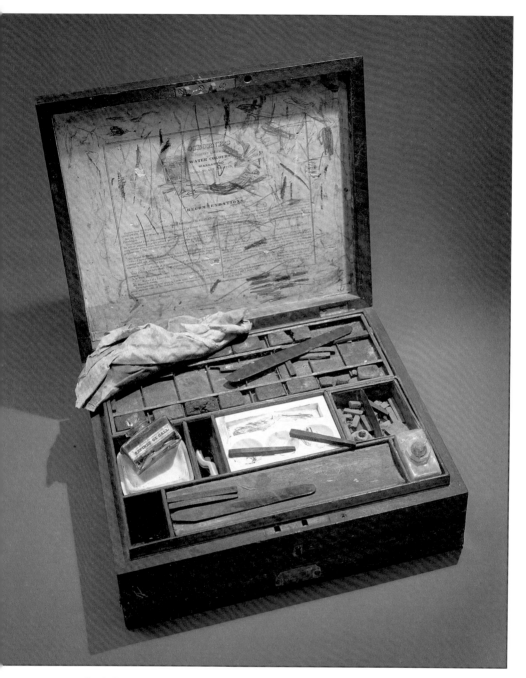

Audubon carried this paintbox, as well as pieces of canvas, with him as he traveled so that he could illustrate birds and other wildlife on the spot.

second daughter, the newborn Rose, was sickly, too, and would die before her first birthday. Child mortality was high in the early nineteenth century. Most families buried at least one child under the age of two. Nevertheless, Audubon mourned his daughters deeply, clearly remembering their "lovely features" even in his old age.

## THE PURSUIT OF A DREAM

When the stress of drawing portraits became too much for him, Audubon went off into the woods in search of birds. He felt a renewed commitment to his bird drawing, something he described as "almost a mania." He needed the wilderness as much as he needed air, water, or even his beloved Lucy. The solitude he found there, he said, "never failed to bring me the most valuable of thoughts, and always comfort. . . ."

The Audubons began to rebuild their lives. Lucy decided she would take up tutoring pupils again. Audubon spent every spare moment adding to his portfolio of birds. He knew he had no real future in painting portraits, but his bird drawings had become better than ever. "Misfortune," he concluded, "had . . . developed my abilities." He was now convinced he could earn a living as an artist.

In the winter of 1820, he learned that Dr. Daniel Drake of Cincinnati had just established a natural history museum. Seeing the very opportunity he had been seeking, Audubon asked an influential friend to write a letter of recommendation. The letter was sent and Audubon received an invitation from Drake to work as a taxidermist and mural painter at the museum for a salary of $125 a month.

Drake gave Audubon the professional encouragement he needed. That spring he organized the first public exhibition of Audubon's drawings and singled out Audubon as "one of the excellent artists attached to the Museum" in his speech at the museum's opening ceremony. A review in the *Cincinnati Inquisitor* also praised Audubon's exhibit as "very superior."

Major Stephen Long, head of the Long Expedition to the western territories, admired Audubon's work, too. The expedition had stopped briefly in Cincinnati as it headed towards the upper reaches of the Missouri River. Audubon would have loved to join it, but Long had already hired a staff artist.

As Audubon watched Long's steamboat, the *Western Engineer*, depart from the Cincinnati docks, a new ambition seized hold of him. He would mount his own expedition. He had been drawing birds for 15 years and had several hundred specimens from the area that encompassed the states of Pennsylvania, Kentucky, Ohio, and Missouri. If he wanted to publish a book, however, he needed birds from an even wider range of territory.

In the summer of 1820, he wrote to Henry Clay, the U.S. Representative from Kentucky, declaring his intention to "explore the territories southwest of the Mississippi" as a professional naturalist on behalf of the United States. All his images, he said, would be life size and would include plants and trees from each bird's natural habitat.

Money, as always, was a problem. Clay was willing to write a letter of introduction for Audubon, but he offered no financial support. The Cincinnati Museum had run out of funds and owed him several months' salary. Lucy had opened a private school in Cincinnati, but this brought only a small income. Audubon helped her when he could by tutoring students in art for an additional fee. Though they could barely survive on what they earned, they were both firmly convinced that Audubon had to pursue his dream.

On October 12, 1820, Audubon boarded the keelboat that would take him on the first leg of his expedition. One of Audubon's best art students, 18-year-old James Mason, joined him. Audubon would hunt game to pay for his passage; Mason would serve as chief cook and bottle washer to pay for his.

Besides the clothes he wore, Audubon took with him his gun, violin, flute, art supplies, one journal, two waterproof wooden portfolios full of drawings, and a well-thumbed book on birds written by the great Swedish biologist Carl Linnaeus. The book was one of his most precious possessions, for it served as his only written source for identifying birds.

## CARL LINNAEUS (1707–1778): THE GREAT CLASSIFIER

Every time we use the words *genus* and *species*, we pay tribute to the Swedish naturalist Carl Linnaeus, whom many historians call the father of taxonomy. *Taxonomy* is another word for classification. Biological taxonomy is a system of classifying organisms into a hierarchical order according to their relationship to one another.

Born in Uppsala, Sweden, in 1707, Linnaeus began collecting plants as a child. By his teens he had accumulated a large library of specimens. Because doctors at that time made medications from plants, he decided to pursue a career

Swedish botanist Carl Linneaus, seen here at age 25 in Laplander dress, is known as the father of modern taxonomy.

in medicine. When he started his studies at the University of Harderwijk in the Netherlands, he discovered that scientific names consisted of long Latin phrases describing a plant's size, shape, color, growth pattern, and habitat. Imagine having to give someone your address by describing the size and color of your house, the length of your street, and the geography of the land surrounding it. Linnaeus wanted to give each plant an "address" on the tree of life. He started by creating a *binomial*, or two-named system, using the

*(continues)*

*(continued)*

terms *genus* and *species*. In 1735, he published a short pamphlet titled *Systema Naturae* that explained his new approach to scientific nomenclature.

In 1741, Linnaeus became a professor of botany at the University of Uppsala. He took charge of the school's botanical garden and rearranged the plants according to his binomial system. His simple and straightforward classification appealed to students and young scientists. Graduates of his courses traveled all over the globe and sent him specimens from Asia, Africa, Australia, and the Americas. By 1758, Linnaeus had classified 7,700 animals and 4,400 plants.

As he worked, Linnaeus refined his system. Eventually, he divided organisms into two kingdoms: plants and animals. Within the kingdoms, he established classes, which were further divided into orders. After the orders came the genera, and lastly the species.

Linnaeus died in 1778 as one of the most celebrated and widely read naturalists of his age. For nearly 300 years, scientists have continued to rely on his theories of classification. In modern taxonomy, the largest classification for organisms is "life" itself. The hierarchy then descends: domain > kingdom > phylum > class > order > family > genus > species. For instance, the scientific classification of the American bald eagle is *Animalia* > *Chordata* > *Ciconiiformes* > *Accipitridae* > *Halliaeetus* > *Halliaeetus leucocephalus*. *Halliaeetus leucocephalus*, which means "sea-eagle with a white head," is the name Linnaeus gave to the bird in 1766.

Each year, biologists continue to discover new species. In 2009, they named nearly 100 new species, including a giant tropical tree *Lecomtedoxa plumose*, a bright blue deep-sea fish *Chromis abyssus*, and a tiny microbe that lives in hairspray, called *Microbacterium hatanonis*. With every new discovery and name, the work of Carl Linnaeus, the great classifier, lives on.

Audubon was glad to be traveling again. He drew cormorants, winter hawks, mallard ducks, crows, robins (which he called "red-breasted thrushes"), and a buzzard in the process of eating a squirrel. He also drew portraits of the boat's passengers and crew. The captain was so impressed with his likeness that he rewarded Audubon with a gold coin.

As they traveled through Missouri, the boat pulled ashore to trade with a party of Osage. Remembering how much he had admired the tribe during his early days in Kentucky, Audubon wrote to Lucy, "Whenever I meet Indians, I feel the greatness of our Creator in all things."

The only serious disaster he experienced during the journey was the loss of one of his portfolios when changing boats in Natchez, Mississippi. Somehow, one of the boatmen had left it on the dock. Audubon sent several messages back, but no one could locate it. He had to go on to New Orleans with only half of his work. Even worse, the portfolio contained his only image of Lucy. He berated himself for his own carelessness, writing that he had forgotten "that no servant could do for me what I might do for myself." He kept the second portfolio in his sight for the rest of the journey. He would never entrust his work to anyone else again. No matter how long or short the distance he traveled, he would carry his own portfolio upon his back.

## GREENHORNS IN NEW ORLEANS

On January 27, 1821, Audubon and Mason arrived in New Orleans. They found the city to be filled with birds—though not necessarily on the wing. In the market, "Canada geese, snow geese, mergansers, robins, bluebirds, red-winged starlings, tell-tale godwits" and even barred owls hung from butchers' hooks, Audubon wrote, ready to be plucked and cooked. The wild fowl were expensive. A pair of ducks sold for $1.25 and a single goose for $1.50. An owl only cost a quarter, making owl gumbo a favorite food of the poor.

In 1823, at age 38, John James Audubon created this oil color portrait of himself.

Audubon, however, could not even afford owl stew, for he had already had his pockets picked by enterprising thieves. He sought out an acquaintance in the city for help. The man gladly lent him a few coins, but only after informing Audubon that he was a "greenhorn" and warning him to be on his guard. Audubon, who prided himself on his independence, must have bristled at the advice, but he had to admit that New Orleans posed challenges he had never faced on the frontier.

Audubon and Mason moved into a rooming house at 34 Barracks Street for $10 a month. The walls were so thin that they could hear every word their neighbors said. Lacking a hearth for cooking, they hung a cured ham from a nail on the wall, cutting off a slice whenever they felt hungry. The maggots, Audubon joked, were particularly athletic, leaping "50 to 60 times their length" across the table to get at the food.

At night the mosquitoes drove the two men from their room into the streets, where they stayed until dawn playing their flutes. "We sometimes have a painter for company," Audubon wrote to Lucy. "And then we talk of the arts." Enclosed in one of his letters, he also sent Lucy $270 that he had earned painting portraits. Roman Parmar, the British counsel in New Orleans, had hired Audubon to do portraits of his wife and three children. That commission led to several more from wealthy families who wanted portraits to decorate their drawing rooms. Audubon's most remarkable portrait, however, was never seen in polite society. He called the sitter "the fair incognito," the beautiful woman with no name.

One day in February, as Audubon was walking down the Rue du Royale with his portfolio upon his shoulder, a heavily veiled young woman approached him and asked in French if he was the artist sent to America by the French Academy to paint birds. Audubon may have been flattered by her assumption that he came from the famous French Academy, or perhaps he thought she was merely teasing. In either case, he simply replied that he painted birds only for his own pleasure. She then asked if he did portraits. When he said yes, she asked him to meet her at her home on the Rue de l'Amour (French for "Street of Love") a half an hour later. Audubon could not see her face behind her veil, but he did note she had a "fine form."

When he arrived at the designated address, he was "trembling like a leaf." After double-locking the door behind him, she removed her veil, revealing one of the most beautiful faces he had ever seen. Their conversation was brief and to the point.

"Are you married?" she asked.

"Yes," he replied.

"How long?"

"Twelve years."

"Is your wife in the city?"

"No, madam."

She smiled. "I will not hurt you."

Audubon could not stop blushing. To ease his discomfort, she brought him a glass of liquor, which he downed in a single gulp.

Sitting opposite him, she looked him straight in the eye. "Have you ever drawn the full figure?"

"Yes."

"Naked?"

Audubon jumped up speechless. "Had I been shot with a 48 pounder [rifle] through the heart," he later recalled, "my articulating powers could not have been more suddenly stopped."

He left the house and roamed the streets for an hour, thinking about what he should do. Audubon had probably never seen a naked woman other than Lucy. He had never drawn a nude. This was a completely new challenge.

He did not back down. He returned to the house and they got to work. The young woman set two conditions. First, she asked that he make no attempt to learn her name, and if he should discover it, he was to keep it to himself. Second, he was to choose a new rifle from one of the best gunsmiths in the city. That would be his payment.

Audubon agreed to both requests. He went to the house every day for nine days. In the afternoon, a servant would bring in cakes and wine. As he ate, the woman pelted him with questions about his family, his background, his travels, and his work, all the while refusing to answer any of his.

She was obviously well educated and knew something about art. At one point she took Audubon's brush from him and sketched her own figure to teach him a few new perspective and foreshortening techniques. She also liked to add her own touches to his work when he wasn't there. "When I returned every day," Audubon wrote in his journal, "I always found the work much advanced."

After he completed the portrait, she bought him his rifle. It cost $125. On the barrel she had the maker inscribe in French, "Do not refuse this gift from one who is in your debt. May its goodness equal your own." Under the ramming rod an inscription in smaller letters read, "Property of LaForest Audubon."

Audubon later claimed he had learned her name and had it inscribed on a part of the rifle "where I do not believe it will ever be found." It wasn't. Audubon never saw her again and her identity remains unknown.

## HOPES ARE SHY BIRDS

The new rifle was a welcome reward. In the spring of 1821, Audubon received another invitation from a lady—this one far more ordinary. The wife of a plantation owner in an area outside of New Orleans known as Bayou Sarah asked Audubon to tutor her teen-age daughter in art and music. Audubon accepted the offer. He was eager to get out of the city and back into the wilderness. In Bayou Sarah he would have plenty of time to hunt and draw birds when he wasn't teaching.

His spirits were also buoyed by the return of the portfolio he had lost in Natchez on the way to New Orleans. A friend had recognized the battered wooden case and sent it to him. Looking over his old work with a fresh eye, Audubon was struck by how much his painting had changed. He had learned a great deal from the artists he met in New Orleans. He now knew how to layer his watercolors. This made his hues richer and deeper, reflecting the true tones he found in nature.

Over the next two years, Audubon moved back and forth between Bayou Sarah and New Orleans, teaching and painting portraits to earn extra cash. He completed at least 60 new birds and redid many of his earlier pictures.

## BERNARD DE MARIGNY: KEY TO THE IDENTITY OF THE FAIR INCOGNITO?

For more than a century, historians have speculated on the identity of the woman Audubon called the "fair incognito." In his later journals he referred to her as Mrs. André. This may have been a pseudonym, but it has led some researchers to believe she was the mistress of Bernard de Marigny, a local real estate developer and politician.

Marigny had befriended Audubon as a fellow French speaker when Audubon first came to New Orleans. The two men were exactly the same age. Both had been born in 1785 of French parents in French colonies—Audubon in Haiti and Marigny in New Orleans. Yet while Audubon readily became an American, Marigny continued to consider himself a Frenchman and preferred to deal only with his own people.

At the age of 15, Marigny had inherited his father's plantation along with a fortune worth $7 million, making him one of the richest men in North America. By the time he was 20, he had gambled

Lucy joined him in 1822 and opened a school for girls at Beech-wood Plantation. She assumed most of the responsibility for supporting the family in order to free Audubon for his painting. They decided that he would complete 90 birds in 90 days. "Every moment I had to spare," he wrote, "I drew birds for my ornithology in which my Lucy and myself alone have faith."

For three more years he worked daily, adding to his portfolio and improving his techniques. Having seen books with color plates produced by American publishers, Audubon knew he would have to go to England to find a printer worthy of his work.

away the bulk of his money. To pay his debts, he began to sell off his land in small parcels, turning his plantation into the Faubourg Marigny, a neighborhood covering a large area southwest of the French Quarter in New Orleans.

Marigny envisioned the Faubourg as a utopian community and gave the new streets inspiring names such as Music, Great Men, Peace, Poets, and Love. The main thoroughfare, Elysian Fields Avenue, became the first street in New Orleans to connect the city's riverfront with Lake Pontchartrain 5 miles (8 km) away.

Because he did not like Englishmen, Marigny sold his plots to French creoles, Spaniards, and the free blacks called *les gens do couleur* ("the people of color"), many of whom had fled Haiti when Napoleon executed Toussaint Louverture in 1803. Though Faubourg Marigny never became the ideal community Marigny intended, it did evolve into one of the city's first multicultural neighborhoods, a home to artists, writers, and musicians of all backgrounds.

In the late nineteenth century, city officials renamed most of the original streets. The Rue de l'Amour, where Audubon met the fair incognito, no longer exists. The mystery, however, continues.

On May 17, 1826, he set sail from New Orleans aboard the *Delos*, carrying with him more than 400 completed paintings. "Hopes are shy birds that fly at a great distance," he had written when he started his journey to New Orleans. Now he was making yet another journey, and his hopes would need to fly higher and farther than ever before.

# An American Frontiersman in England

Audubon must have made a striking figure when he disembarked in Liverpool, England, on July 21, 1826. At 41 years old, he was tall and broad shouldered and walked with an athletic stride. His long red hair, only lightly tinged with gray, hung loosely over his shoulders. He had gone to America 23 years earlier wearing silks and satins. Now he arrived in Europe clad in the fringed deerskin jacket, leggings, and soft moccasin-style boots of an American frontiersman.

Had he arrived a year earlier, his appearance among the well-tailored Englishmen might have attracted ridicule. In early 1826, however, James Fenimore Cooper's novel of frontier life, *The Last of the Mohicans*, had taken the country by storm. Suddenly, American frontiersmen were the latest rage in English society. When he walked the streets of Liverpool, Audubon wrote to Lucy, "My locks flew freely from under my hat, and every lady that I met looked at them and then at me until she could see no more." Years of living in the woods had not made Audubon vain. He was probably more embarrassed by the stares than flattered. In truth, he felt dreadfully insecure. "I imagined that every individual whom I was about to meet might be possessed of talent superior to those of any

John James Audubon created this pencil-drawn self-portrait at age 41 in 1826.

on our side of the Atlantic," he confided in one of his first letters home.

## PRAISE FOR THE BIRDS

Audubon carried many letters of introduction to Englishmen from friends in America, but the cold reception he received at the first few homes he visited did little to help his insecurity. Only when he called on the family of Richard Rathbone did he find the warm welcome he longed for.

Rathbone, a cotton merchant and social reformer, took an immediate liking to the unorthodox American visitor. Even more importantly, he appreciated Audubon's art. "These friends praised my Birds," Audubon wrote triumphantly in a letter to Lucy. "And I felt the praise." One good word about his paintings meant more to him than all the admiring glances of the most beautiful women in the entire nation.

With Rathbone's support, Audubon mounted an exhibition of his work at Liverpool's Royal Institute. He listened with joy as visitor after visitor declared that the pictures made them wish they were "in the forests of America."

Later, Rathbone's wife, whom Audubon called the Queen Bee, invited her friends to meet Audubon. He played American frontier tunes on his flute and fiddle and entertained them with birdcalls. (The wild turkey hoot was his specialty.)

More exhibits and parties followed. In the space of a few weeks Audubon had gone from feeling utterly alone to being the center of a social whirl. He dined out every night, not coming home until very late. He woke around 9 or 10, wrote and painted for a few hours, and then set off on his round of social calls again.

Back home he had always risen in the early hours before dawn, the best time to observe birds. His new schedule left him anxious and disoriented. "My head is like a hornet's nest and my body wearied beyond all calculation," he wrote. Yet he knew he needed the support of wealthy people to publish his book. "It has to be done," he continued. "I cannot refuse a single invitation."

To a man who had spent most of his life sleeping in log cabins or on the open ground, the estates of British nobility seemed astounding. Audubon couldn't get used to the frequent meals and rich dishes. At home he ate sparingly, sometimes surviving on one meal a day or less. In England every visit he made resulted in an offer of food. "If my friends complain of my not eating much, they must at all events allow that I eat sufficiently often," he wrote to Lucy after sitting down to yet another luncheon of fried oysters, wine, and cake.

At the country estate of Earl and Lady Morton, he stayed in a guestroom that contained a bed big enough for four men, plus a sofa,

## NATTY BUMPPO: AMERICA'S FIRST FRONTIER HERO

Natty Bumppo may sound like a strange name for a romantic hero, but in 1826, Bumppo embodied the American ideal. Strong, silent, loyal, and courageous, he never missed his mark and lived by the motto "one shot, one kill." He made his home in the wilderness, where Native Americans accepted him as a "blood brother." They called him Hawkeye, Deerslayer, Pathfinder, and Long Rifle. Like any true hero, he was always ready to fight for truth and justice.

He was also completely imaginary. James Fenimore Cooper created Bumppo in *Leatherstocking Tales*, his series of novels about the early American frontier that he published between 1823 and 1841. The second book, *The Last of the Mohicans: A Narrative of 1757*, features Bumppo and his Mohican friend Chingachgook in a plot of hair-raising escapades set against the backdrop of the French and Indian War.

two armchairs, a table, desk, and "all that I never use anywhere," he wrote. Wandering down the hall on his way to dinner, he opened a door out of curiosity and discovered "a neat little closet" equipped with a porcelain tub, jars of water, soap, linen cloths, and thick towels. It was, he realized with amazement, a room just for bathing. He examined everything, but "touched nothing," concluding that he was "clean enough" already.

He peeked inside another door and found a second closet, "differently intended." He doesn't elaborate any further, but it is likely that it was a "water closet," or toilet, operated by a flushing mechanism on a long chord. Again, Audubon doesn't say when or whether

*Mohicans* became a best-seller on both sides of the Atlantic. Within a few years, translations appeared in French, German, Dutch, Italian, Danish, Norwegian, and Russian. When Cooper arrived in England with his family in 1826, British fans greeted him as a celebrity.

Contemporary historians have criticized Cooper's stereotypes of Native Americans. Though he did know some Mohican and Iroquois while growing up in New York State, Cooper did not possess any real knowledge of Native American rituals and traditions. In his defense, it can be said that most of his white characters, including Natty Bumppo, are stereotypes, too.

Despite their many flaws, Cooper's novels have shaped the popular image of the American frontier for nearly two centuries. Between 1909 and 1996, more than 30 films and 7 television series based on the Natty Bumppo stories were produced in Hollywood and abroad. In 2007, Marvel Comics released a graphic novel of *The Last of the Mohicans*, illustrated by Stephen Kurth and written by Roy Thomas, author of Marvel's other great adventures *Conan the Barbarian*, *The Avengers*, and *Classic X-Men*.

he used it, though it was no doubt one of his most novel experiences in all of England.

## THROUGH THE EYES OF AN EAGLE

For the next several months, Audubon toured the cities of Manchester, Newcastle, Glasgow, and Edinburgh, exhibiting his pictures and gathering subscribers for his book. As he traveled, he became aware of how much land had been cleared in England to make way for factories and mills. In America, the wilderness seemed vast and endless. Audubon, like most of his fellow citizens, had never stopped to think it might one day be gone. Now he saw proof that the forests would not last forever. "Neither this little stream, this swamp, this grand sheet of flowing water, nor these mountains will be seen in a century," he wrote of America in his journal:

> The currents will be tormented and turned astray from their primitive courses. The hills will be leveled with the swamp . . . Scarce a magnolia will Louisiana possess. The timid deer will exist no more. Fishes will no longer bask on the surface, the eagle scarce ever alight, and these millions of songsters will be drove away by man.

Audubon had no way of knowing how true or false his prophecy would be, but the idea that human activities could demolish nature permanently gave a new urgency to his need to publish *Birds of America*.

In Edinburgh, Audubon presented a public lecture at a meeting of the Wernerian Natural History Society. Sitting in the audience was a 19-year-old medical student named Charles Darwin. Darwin was intrigued by Audubon's comments on the birds of the New World. Birds would become key to his own research and he would cite Audubon's work several times in his pioneering book *On the Origin of Species*, published in 1859.

Audubon had his portrait done in Edinburgh by the Scottish artist John Syme. He posed in his wolfskin jacket with his rifle cradled

# CHARLES DARWIN'S FINCHES

When Darwin returned from his voyage to the Galapagos Islands in 1836, he brought with him several finches. The birds looked nearly identical, being small and gray with short tails and rounded wings. The only thing that distinguished them from one another was the beak. Some had long, narrow beaks, others short, wide beaks, and still others beaks of various sizes in between.

The Galapagos Islands form an archipelago that stretches across nearly 28,000 square miles (72,500 sq. km) of the Pacific Ocean near the Equator off the western coast of South America. The archipelago consists of 28 islands plus at least 107 small outcroppings of rock and soil called islets. Darwin visited the islands between 1831 and 1835. He noticed that the finches on each island had a different diet. Warbler finches used their sharp, pointed beaks to hunt insects. Cactus finches used their long, narrow beaks to probe seeds from the inside of cactus fruit. Ground finches used their wide, thick beaks to crack hard-shelled seeds found on the ground.

In his journal Darwin wrote, "Seeing the diversity of beaks and other structures in the closely related finches, one might really fancy that one species had been taken and modified for different ends." Upon arriving in England, he shared his finch specimens with the ornithologist John Gould. After studying the finches, Gould told Darwin that the finches of each island had apparently been "modified" so much they were actually 14 different species.

Darwin had been thinking about a process he called "the transmutation of species." If finches needed a certain kind of beak to take advantage of the food source on a particular island, he reasoned, only the finches with that type of beak would be able to survive and breed. The different kinds of beaks represented an adaptation to a unique environment.

*(continues)*

*(continued)*

Darwin did not know about genetics, so he had no clear idea exactly how changes in beak shape and size were passed from generation to generation. In 2006, researchers from Harvard Medical School unraveled a crucial piece of this puzzle. They had received permission from the government of Ecuador to take physiological samples from finch eggs on the Galapagos, and they discovered that the finches generated a calcium-binding protein called calmodulin. The long-beaked cactus finch had more calmodulin than the short-beaked ground finch. This led to the hypothesis that calmodulin serves as a trigger for the genes that control beak shape and length.

Additional research may reveal ways in which calmodulin influences the development of mammal skulls, including those of human beings. After 170 years, Darwin's finches are still making evolutionary news.

in his arms, looking out into the distance just as he did when he went hunting in the woods. When he saw the finished painting, he expressed surprise at the intensity of his gaze. His eyes, he wrote to his friend the Queen Bee, seemed "more those of an enraged eagle than mine." He underestimated his charisma. Everyone who knew him commented on how well the portrait captured his spirit. The painting has been reproduced thousands of times. It was donated to the White House in the early 1960s and put on permanent display in the Red Room.

## *Ze Jig is Up!*

By 1827, Audubon had collected more than a hundred subscriptions for his book. He planned to issue the *Birds of America* in a series of

Audubon sat with his rifle in hand to have this portrait painted by British artist John Syme. It is now part of a collection on display in the White House.

"numbers," each containing five color plates. Five numbers would be sent to the subscribers every year. A single volume would be made up of 20 numbers. Audubon wanted to print 300 separate images, which meant the entire project would encompass 60 numbers and take at least 12 years. To present the birds as life size, the printer would use the largest grade of paper, called "double elephant." Each volume would measure 26½ by 39 inches (67 by 99 cm) and weigh about 40 pounds (18 kg).

The completed work became known as *The Audubon Elephant Folio*. The name is still used today and sometimes leads readers unfamiliar with Audubon to assume the book contains pictures of elephants, though it only refers to the size of the paper.

In the prospectus he sent out to potential subscribers, Audubon assured them that "the author has not contented himself with single profile views of the originals, but in very many instances he has grouped them, as it were, at their natural avocations, in all sorts of attitudes." He presented his birds in their natural habitats, swimming, gliding, singing, fighting, sitting on their nests, feeding their young, foraging for food, or swooping down upon their prey. *Birds of America* would be, he claimed, "one of the most splendid publications which has ever appeared."

Audubon contracted a printer in Edinburgh in the winter of 1827, but the first samples of their work failed to impress him so he went to London in search of better craftsmen. Friends referred him to Robert Havell Sr., one of the city's most well-respected engravers. Havell was also an amateur zoologist and felt an instant kinship with Audubon

Havell and his son Robert Havell Jr. produced a sample for Audubon's approval. Havell Jr., who later became a close friend of Audubon, liked to recount the story of Audubon's first look at the finished engraving: He began to dance around the printer's studio shouting, "Ze jig is up! Ze jig is up!!" The Havells thought he was angry, until he threw his arms around them and they realized he was telling them that he was so happy with their work he could dance a jig.

In this 1949 image, students admire the large-scale elephant folio *Birds of America*. Unique for its size and detail, the book and, even separately, the images in it have been popular reference materials since their inception.

## AUDUBON AND LUCY: APART AND TOGETHER AGAIN

While all this was going on, Audubon's relationship with Lucy had become incredibly strained. He had been in England for nearly three years. The two had never been separated so long. Audubon wanted Lucy to come to England. Lucy wanted the man she called "her LaForest" to come home. When she wrote to him about all the new friends she had made teaching school in Louisiana, he felt she did not care about his work anymore. When he wrote about his success abroad, she felt he had lost interest in his family. Delays in transatlantic mail delivery did not help matters. Letters might not arrive for months, or they might arrive in the wrong order. Misunderstandings piled up.

Audubon did not like living in England, yet he was reluctant to leave until the printing of *Birds of America* was complete. That, however, could take another decade. He and Lucy had been together for more than 20 years, and now he feared they were falling apart. At his lowest point he wrote, "I sometimes fear we shall never meet again in this world."

Victor, the Audubon's eldest son, now 18, was attending school in Cincinnati and found himself playing referee between his parents. Each wrote him letters detailing the faults of the other. Somehow he managed to bring them together. At the very moment Lucy decided to leave for England, Audubon declared he was coming home to fetch her. No amount of recognition and success meant anything to him if Lucy was not there to share it. "Honors—hopes of wealth," he had once told her, "is all in my soul for thy sake and thine own sake only."

On April 1, 1829, Audubon boarded a ship leaving Portsmouth, England, for New York. He was nearly 44 and Lucy 40. "We have been married a good time," he wrote. "And circumstances have caused our voyage to become mottled with incidents of a very different nature." If she was willing to return to England with him, he told her, their voyage together would resume.

# Fame at Last:
# Audubon the
# Ornithologist

Audubon arrived in New York on May 6, 1829. He immediately noticed how much the landscape had changed during his three years abroad. Economic progress had come to the United States. In northeastern Pennsylvania, he stopped for several days at a place called the Great Pine Forest on the banks of the Lehigh River, where a lumber sawmill had been constructed. "Trees one after another were heard . . . falling in the days," he wrote. "And in the calm nights the greedy mills told the tale that in a century the noble forests around would exist no more."

During a brief visit to Philadelphia he expressed surprise that so few people in the city had even heard of the Pine Forest. Philadelphians, he complained, preferred to see nature in the glass cases of Charles Wilson Peale's Natural History Museum. Audubon himself had worked for a natural history museum and he relied on the curators of those institutions to support his work. He had nothing against museums, but he believed nature could best be appreciated in the wild.

On the last leg of his journey, Audubon traveled down the Ohio River to the Mississippi by steamboat. As the boat passed Louisville, he recalled his first days on the frontier 20 years earlier. This time he encountered few Native Americans hunting along the banks and the "vast herds of deer elk and buffalo" were almost gone. Everywhere he looked he saw new settlements. Whole towns had sprung up. "The din of hammers and machinery is constantly heard," he noted in his journal. Audubon did not think progress was in itself bad. He didn't want to ban settlements. He simply wanted to make sure there was a record of the wilderness that existed when the first settlers came.

## PEALE'S PHILADELPHIA MUSEUM

On July 18, 1786, Charles Wilson Peale of Philadelphia opened the first museum in the United States. Peale was already famous for his many portraits of Revolutionary War heroes. His new museum, however, did not display paintings, but rather "objects of natural history and things useful and curious." Among his most popular specimens were a stuffed bison, a 5-foot-long (1.5-m-long) preserved freshwater paddlefish called a "monster," and a pair of pheasants shot and donated by George Washington.

Peale posted ads in newspapers asking people to send him "precious curiosities from many parts of the world." By 1799, the collection included 100 mammals, 700 birds, 150 amphibians, and thousands of insects, plants, and small fossils. He exhibited the first anteater seen by North Americans and a "camel-leopard" from Africa, otherwise known as a giraffe.

In 1801, Peale added an even more spectacular item to his collection: A nearly complete mastodon skeleton that had been

Audubon finally joined Lucy in New Orleans in November 1829. While she finished her teaching for the semester, he drew and collected specimens for his friends in England, including 14 live possums that he shipped to the London Zoo.

## THE AUDUBONS ABROAD

The Audubons left Louisiana in March. On their way to New York, they stopped in Washington, D.C., where Audubon presented an exhibit of his drawings in the Capitol Building. Afterwards the House of Representatives voted to buy a subscription to *Birds of*

unearthed in Hudson, New York. With the assistance of his friend Caspar Wistar, a professor of anatomy from the University of Pennsylvania, Peale reconstructed the skeleton for his museum. His finished mastodon measured 11 feet (3.3 m) high and 17 feet (5 m) long. When the museum moved to Independence Hall, the mastodon occupied an entire room.

An educator as well as a showman, Peale used the Linnaean system of classification to label his specimens and developed new methods of taxidermy to present his animals in natural poses. Though Audubon never exhibited his own work at Peale's museum, he surely visited it several times when he first came to Pennsylvania in 1803.

Peale died in 1827. His sons took over the museum for several years, eventually selling the collection in the 1840s. A large portion of it went to P.T. Barnum. The mastodon skeleton no longer exists, but a painting Peale did of the excavation, *Exhuming the Mastodon*, is owned by the Maryland Historical Society and is on permanent exhibition at the society's Baltimore museum.

*America* on behalf of the government. It was the only federal support Audubon ever received for his work.

On April 27, 1830, they departed from New York for London. Audubon brought with him 350 live passenger pigeons, which he had purchased in the city for four cents each. It is not known how many of the birds survived the journey.

In England, Audubon was pleased to learn he had been elected a member of the Royal Sociey of London, Britain's most prestigious scientific society. Lucy rejoiced to see her husband honored. Audubon seldom spoke of his hunger for public recognition. On many occasions he dismissed fame as something that would come only after his death. Lucy, who had seen him struggle through bankruptcy and defeat, knew how much he valued this sign of acceptance from England's most learned scholars.

Audubon had another surprise for Lucy. Before he had left England he had asked Havell to engrave "Drawn from Nature by Lucy Audubon" on a plate showing a picture of a swamp sparrow perched on a blossoming mayapple branch. The image of the delicate bird must have been one of Lucy's favorites. She had not drawn it, of course, but Audubon was paying her the greatest compliment he knew. She had been part of his book from the beginning and now her name would be in it, too.

On his first trip to England, several of his supporters had suggested to Audubon that he write a book about birds to accompany his pictures. Though Audubon had kept journals all his adult life, he had never considered himself a professional writer. Undaunted, he started his new project with the same enthusiasm and self-discipline that characterized his drawing. He called the book *Ornithological Biographies*. To make sure it was up to London's literary standards, he hired a young ornithologist he had met in Edinburgh, William MacGillivray, to act as his editor. "Writing now became the order of the day," he told his sons in a letter. He rose at four in the morning and kept writing until evening. "So full was my mind of birds and their habits that in my sleep I continually dreamed of birds," he recalled.

Audubon had this image of a swamp sparrow specially engraved
and credited to his wife, Lucy, in *Birds of America*.

*Ornithological Biographies* would become a monumental work in itself, running more than a thousand pages. It was not just a book on birds, but Audubon's autobiography as well, for woven into the essays on ornithology were "anecdotes and adventures" from his own life.

Audubon was not above embroidering the truth here and there. He wrote about a hunting trip with Daniel Boone that could not have possibly taken place. Boone was well into his seventies when Audubon arrived in Kentucky in 1808 and his hunting days were over. This doesn't mean the book was based on lies, though. Few nineteenth-century memoirs were entirely free of name-dropping or dramatized incidents. Readers expected a little romance with their history. Perhaps Audubon thought he was merely satisfying the European desire to see him as the ideal frontiersman. The Boone episode aside, most of what Audubon wrote was indeed true. His encounters with the Shawnee and Osage, his trips down the Mississippi, and his days in the cypress forests of the bayous had occurred as he described them. He had once bemoaned the lack of a record of the wilderness in the early days of the United States; now he had created that record himself for the world to read.

## I WILL LEAVE NO PLACE UNSEARCHED

Havell, Audubon's engraver, completed the first volume of *Birds of America* in December 1830, nearly a year ahead of schedule. Once Audubon could see that his work was in good hands and the printing could proceed without his daily supervision, he made plans to return to the United States. He and Lucy were, after all, Americans. They may have enjoyed England, but only the United States could ever be home.

Besides, Audubon knew he had a lot of work to do. His books still lacked many birds from the south, far north, and west of the country. He began to plan expeditions to Florida, Nova Scotia, and the territories beyond the Mississippi. Many men of Audubon's era considered themselves old at 40, yet at 46 Audubon showed no signs of slowing down. "I am going to America," he wrote to a friend. "And I assure you that if life is granted to me I will leave no place in the U.S. unsearched." He was ready for the wilderness again.

## SOUTH TO CHARLESTON AND FLORIDA

The Audubons returned to the United States in September 1831. Victor, relieved to see his parents back together, met them in New York. He then took Lucy to Louisville, where she would stay with her brother William while Audubon traveled south. Once more they were separated. "I miss you," Lucy wrote the minute she arrived in Louisville. "But on this journey I know how much your success and fame depends. The world has its eyes upon you, my dear LaForest."

Audubon was no longer an unknown backwoodsman. Lucy's LaForest had become a celebrated ornithologist. Audubon's fame preceded him at Charleston. When he arrived in the South Carolina city, a friend introduced him to the southern naturalist John Bachman. Bachman greeted Audubon as a celebrity and insisted Audubon and his companions stay at his home, a luxurious mansion that must have reminded Audubon of his father's old house in Haiti.

If he was pleased with his new status, however, Audubon had the sense to wear his fame lightly. "I jumped at once into my wood-hunting habits," he wrote to Lucy. That meant rising at three in the morning and hunting until noon, usually with nothing more than water and a few biscuits spread with molasses for refreshment. After a more substantial lunch, he would mount his newly shot specimens, draw, and write until evening. Sometimes he would go out again after dark for several hours to observe nocturnal birds. This was the life he loved best.

Sometimes a hunting expedition took more than one day. Then dinner would be prepared over an open fire. "We had no cook, save your humble servant," he wrote of one such meal. "The oyster and fish were thrown on the embers and the steaks put on sticks in front." The campers had forgotten to bring salt, but Audubon quickly showed them how to use gunpowder, which was made from saltpeter, as a substitute, something he had done many times before. Lacking forks or plates, their fingers became black with charcoal and gunpowder. The steaks, Audubon said, were as savory as any cooked at home, and better, he might have added, than any served on china platters.

## Florida: Mud and Sand

In the winter of 1832, Audubon made his first trip to Florida. He swore he would explore the Everglades "or die in the attempt."

"All that is not mud, mud, mud," he wrote, "is sand, sand, sand." Everywhere he looked he saw "alligators, scorpions, and snakes." Fearlessly, he waded waist-deep through the swamps. Alligators, he had learned during his days in Louisiana, seldom attacked human beings. The best way to deflect a gator was to approach the beast head on and rap it smartly on the skull with a stick about 4 feet (1.2 m) long. The real danger came not from the jaws, but from the powerful tail. As long as you avoided the thrashing of the tail, he claimed, you could proceed unharmed.

Only once did Audubon see an alligator killed. On Florida's St. Johns River, a sailor shot a large gator following their boat. Alligator brains scattered through the air and the river ran red with blood. The dying gator thrashed furiously, sinking out of sight before Audubon could retrieve the body for study.

Traveling through the pine barrens he discovered cormorants, herons, fish hawks, eagles, crows, gannets, white ibises, and flamingos "advancing in an 'Indian Line' with well-spread wings, outstretched necks, and long legs directed backwards." The sight of the big pink birds must have changed Audubon's opinion of Florida for the better, for he wrote, "I had now reached the height of my expectation."

He loved wild orange groves and the "golden fruit" that quenched his thirst almost instantly. Oranges were so plentiful that people in Florida fed them to their horses. The horses, Audubon noted, ate them "with relish." Settlers also pressed the oranges in wooden mills and sold the juice in barrels. "The very air you breathe in such a place invigorates you," he wrote. Florida was indeed a garden, not just a swamp.

The garden, though, had begun to lose most of its original inhabitants. In the Everglades, a young Seminole man in a canoe approached Audubon's boat, offering to trade his catch of fish and birds for gunpowder. He made his trade and left without a smile or word of any kind. He had reason to distrust the visitors. The Seminole Wars had killed many of his people and forced most of the survivors to lands west of Mississippi. By the time Audubon arrived in Florida in 1832, the Seminole had lost almost all of their traditional lands.

Audubon watched the young man row away with sadness: "The poor, dejected son of the woods endowed with talents of the highest order, though rarely acknowledged by the proud usurpers of his land," he wrote. "Would that I could restore to thee thy birthright, thy natural independence." Audubon had long respected the culture of Native Americans, even if other white men did not.

## NORTH TO LABRADOR

Audubon left Florida in the summer of 1832. He arrived in Boston in October to prepare for his expedition northward through the Bay of Fundy and around the Gulf of Saint Lawrence to Newfoundland. His younger son, John Woodhouse, would be traveling with him. At 20, John Woodhouse was an excellent artist. He would help mount specimens and add background touches to Audubon's drawings.

Audubon and John Woodhouse spent the winter buying supplies. On the morning of March 16, 1833, a month from their departure date, Audubon woke to find he could not move his hands. When he tried to call for help, he couldn't speak. Though he didn't know it, he had suffered a stroke. Lucy was with him at the time and called for a doctor. The doctor attributed the illness to overwork. Audubon was not quite 48 years old, and he had always enjoyed excellent health. Through sheer willpower, he pulled himself together. Four days later, he was back to writing in his journal. Moderate exercise and less work, he hoped, would cure any lingering disability.

Audubon's idea of moderation still meant doing more in one day than most men did in a week. After a brief trip down to New York to drop Lucy off with friends, Audubon and his son headed up to Eastport, Maine, in early June. Four additional young men joined them there aboard the schooner the *Ripley,* which would be their home for the next three months.

Before they set off for Canada, they took a brief excursion to Grand Manan Island, 10 miles (16 km) off the coast of Maine. In the company of men half his age, Audubon went rappelling down the rocky cliffs to examine ravens' nests. "I am Audubon again!" he declared. His strength restored, he faced the next adventure armed, as always, with his gun and pen.

## The Bird Rock

As the ship moved through the Bay of Fundy, Audubon sighted Blackburnian warblers, piping plovers, Eskimo curlews, gulls, and puffins. The waters teemed with fish, including cod, mackerel, herring, and halibut. Lobsters were so plentiful that all the fishermen had to do to catch them was dip an oar into the water and let the lobsters grab hold.

The highlight of the trip came when the ship passed a small island called a "bird rock." It appeared to be covered with several feet of snow. Audubon examined the island through a small telescope. "I rubbed my eyes," he wrote in his *Labrador Journal,* "took my spyglass, and in an instant the strangest picture stood before me. They were birds we saw, a mass of birds of such a size as I never before cast my eyes on." The "snow" was actually thousands of northern gannets. These large, white, seagull-like sea birds came to nest on the rock every year.

The birds showed little fear of humans. Upon landing on the island, Audubon walked among them and noted that the rocky ground was blanketed with nests arranged in neat rows, much like a crop of cabbage or sweet potatoes.

Local fishermen used gannet flesh as codfish bait. Audubon witnessed six men from nearby Halifax club more than 500 birds to death in the space of an hour. He called the carnage "murder." To add insult to injury, he said, the birds were carelessly skinned and the unwanted carcasses left to rot. "The stench from the rock is insufferable," he wrote a few days later. "As it is covered with the remains of putrid fish, rotting eggs, and dead birds, young and old." Audubon had hunted birds all his life, but he was careful not to kill more than he needed.

Even more outrageous than overhunting was the practice of "egging." While observing a nesting colony of wild geese, Audubon saw groups of men gathering eggs by the hundreds. These "eggers" sold their booty to merchants, who then transported the haul to towns and cities. A dozen goose eggs could be purchased in Halifax or Quebec for 25 cents.

Egging was a major maritime industry. Audubon learned that four men had gathered 40,000 goose eggs the previous spring. Twenty ships deployed teams of eggers off the coast of Halifax, resulting in a haul of at least 800,000 eggs each season in that area of Labrador alone.

Audubon was quick to point out the devastating consequences of killing off future generations. Female birds robbed of one set of eggs would continue to lay again and again until exhausted, all without raising a single nestling. "In less than a half-century these wonderful nurseries will be entirely destroyed," he wrote, "unless some kind government will interfere to stop this destruction."

The idea that the government could step in to save birds was a new one. Audubon may not have been the first to suggest it, but he was certainly among the earliest and strongest supporters of legal protection for wildlife. Before he left Labrador, Audubon had dinner aboard a French-Canadian vessel making a survey of the coast. The ship's captain was a naturalist himself and the two men engaged in a long discussion on the current state of Labrador:

We talked of the country where we were of the beings best fitted to live and prosper here, not only our species, but of all species, and also of the enormous destruction here of everything except the rocks, the aborigines themselves melting away before the encroachments of the white man, who looks without pity upon the decrease of the devoted Indian from whom he rifles home, food, clothing and life . . . Nature herself seems to be perishing . . . When no more fish, no more game, no more birds exist on her hills, along her coasts and in her rivers, then she will be abandoned and deserted like a worn out field.

Audubon must have known that he was talking not just of Labrador, but about his own country, too. He returned to the United States in September 1833 with a portfolio of northern birds and a greater appreciation for the fragility of the wilderness he loved.

## THE LAST EXPEDITIONS

Though nearly 50 and suffering from bouts of ill health, Audubon refused to slacken his pace. Between 1834 and 1844, he made two trips to England and two expeditions in the United States. The first U.S. expedition was in 1837 to the Gulf Coast and Galveston, Texas, and the second was in 1840 to the Missouri territories west of the Mississippi, an area that included the present-day states of Iowa, Nebraska, South Dakota, and eastern Kansas.

On November 9, 1836, Audubon and his son John Woodhouse dined at the White House with President Andrew Jackson. Audubon avoided talking about politics, but did note that the president "seemed adverse to the cause of Texas." Texas had just declared itself an independent republic on March 6, 1836. A year later, on May 15, 1837, Audubon and his son met the republic's president, Sam Houston. Audubon found Houston an impressive, if somewhat stern leader. They drank a cup of grog together. Audubon, ever a champion of freedom, raised a toast to the success of the new nation-state.

When Audubon's *Birds of America* was being published, Andrew Jackson was campaigning for the office of U.S. president. Once he became president, Jackson, who sat for this watercolor lithograph in 1830, invited Audubon and his son to the White House.

Audubon's illustration of an American bison was colored in 1845, two years after his final expedition.

The fifth and final volume of *Birds of America* was finished on June 16, 1838. The total work included 435 hand-colored prints of 1,065 individual birds. Audubon barely took time to celebrate. In 1839, he launched a major project on North American mammals, *Viviparous Quadrupeds of North America,* with his friend John Bachman. They hoped *Quadrupeds* would become a companion piece to *Birds.*

In the spring of 1843, Audubon departed on what was to become his final expedition. Along with four fellow naturalists, he boarded the steamboat *Omega* in St. Louis, Missouri, for an excursion upriver to the Dakotas. When the boat reached the Platt River

# SCOTTY PHILIP'S BISON

Historians estimate that there were more than 40 million American bison in the United States in 1800. Between 1830 and 1885, almost all of them were killed. The last great "buffalo" hunt took place at Grand River, South Dakota, in 1881. Pete Dupree, a South Dakota rancher, rescued five calves from the slaughter and brought them back to his spread. Fifteen years later he had a small herd of about 50 animals. When Dupree died around 1899, a neighboring rancher, Scotty Philip, purchased the bison from Dupree's nephew.

Philip launched a serious breeding program. He set aside a stretch of pasture along the banks of the Missouri River, where the herd would have a safe place to graze. As the number increased, zoos and national parks began asking Philip for breeding stock. By 1910, he had more than a thousand bison—the largest herd in the world. People called him "the buffalo king."

Philip died at the age of 53 in 1911. According to the local newspaper, his bison came down from the hills to watch the funeral procession pass by along the road. In the 1920s, Philip's family donated his herd to South Dakota's Custer State Park.

As of 2008, there were about 15,000 wild American bison living in parks and protected lands throughout the United States. Almost all were descended from Philip's original herd. Ranchers continue to raise domestic bison, which numbered around a half-million in 2010.

Every September, Custer State Park sponsors an annual bison round-up. The event has become one of South Dakota's biggest tourist attractions, a chance for visitors to catch a brief glimpse of what the West was like back in the days when the buffalo really did roam.

in southeast Nebraska, Audubon caught his first glimpse of the Great Plains. At Fort Union, the crew and passengers of the ship disembarked to hunt buffalo (the often-used colloquial name for American bison). The herd numbered in the thousands, covering the prairie in every direction. Yet even that was small, Audubon learned, compared to the vast herds trappers had encountered only 20 years earlier. He called the American bison "a noble animal" whose worst enemy was man.

## "I WOULD FLY OFF…"

Audubon's interest in nature was as keen as ever, but he spent more time on the prairie observing than he did hunting and hiking. He had finally begun to slow down.

The first volume of *Quadrupeds* appeared in 1846. Audubon would not live to see it through to completion. In 1847, his memory started to fail. Lucy noticed that "the brightness of his eye" had begun to dim. He had what is now known to be Alzheimer's disease.

The Audubons were living on an estate in the unsettled region of upper Manhattan overlooking the Hudson River. Audubon had named it Minnie's Land, after his pet name for Lucy. John Bachman came to visit in 1848 and wrote to his family, "The countenance & his general robust form are there, but the mind is all in ruins."

Audubon died peacefully in his sleep at the age of 65 on January 27, 1851. He was buried in Trinity Cemetery in New York City. Lucy survived him by 23 years. She died in 1874 and was buried beside him.

During his lifetime, Audubon had hunted with Native Americans and dined with presidents. He waded through tropical swamps and sailed through iceberg-filled seas. Cities as diverse as New York, Philadelphia, Louisville, and New Orleans claimed him as one of their own. He had survived earthquakes and financial ruin, fought his enemies single-handedly, and befriended some

In his later years, John James Audubon, shown here in his 60s, was much less active as he suffered from senility due to what is now known as Alzheimer's disease. He died at age 65.

of the greatest scientists of his age. Through it all he loved one woman, drew thousands of pictures, and filled thousands of pages with his words. Most important, he had sounded the alarm about the destruction of the wilderness long before others even thought such a thing possible.

In his introduction to *Birds of America,* he wrote of his days in the woods:

Although her husband was an artist, few images exist of Audubon's wife, Lucy. She died long after him, but was buried beside him in Trinity Cemetery at 155th Street and Broadway in New York City, not far from where they once lived.

The sky was serene, the air perfumed and thousands of melodious notes from birds all unknown to me urged me to arise and go in pursuit of those beautiful and happy creatures. Then I would find myself furnished with large and powerful wings and, cleaving the air like an eagle, I would fly off . . .

He was a hero in every sense of the word.

# The Audubon Society: Audubon's Legacy

One afternoon in 1896, Harriet Hemenway, Minna Hall, Jennie June Croly, and several other Boston ladies did something very unusual. They stopped wearing their hats. In the 1890s, American women wore elaborate hats festooned with feathers, feathers, and more feathers. Sometimes a hat displayed an entire bird on the crown. Egrets, owls, bluebirds, woodpeckers, Baltimore orioles, and hummingbirds were particularly popular decorations. A few years earlier, New York ornithologist Frank Chapman had spotted no fewer than 132 different species of birds on women's heads while strolling down a Manhattan street.

The Boston women replaced their fancy hats with plainer straw, felt, or wool versions. They had just formed the Massachusetts Audubon Society and wanted to prove to their fashionable friends that they could be elegant without exploiting birds.

George Grinnel, editor of the magazine *Forest and Stream*, had founded the first Audubon Society in New York in 1886. The new

*(continues on page 116)*

# ORNITHOLOGY FOR EVERYONE: ROGER TORY PETERSON

When Blanche Hornbeck started a chapter of the Junior Audubon Society for her seventh grade class in the fall of 1919, she had no idea she was going to change the life of one of her students forever.

Eleven-year-old Roger Tory Peterson had always loved exploring the woods around his home in Jamestown, New York. With one of Miss Hornbeck's Audubon brochures in hand, he set off on a bird-watching expedition that very afternoon. A golden brown northern flicker flew by. Peterson made his very first bird identification. From that moment on he was hooked on birds.

Soon he started getting up at two in the morning so he could identify birds while working on his newspaper route. He used his earnings to buy a camera and binoculars. All winter he skied through the snow-covered fields to keep 20 feeding stations filled with birdseed. His only difficulty was finding a book that would enable him to easily and accurately identify birds from a distance.

After graduating from high school in 1925, Peterson moved to New York to study art. There, he joined the Bronx Bird Watchers Club, led by Ludlow Griscom, author of *Birds of New York City and Region*. Griscom didn't consider bird watching a pastime only for the educated elite; he regarded it as a popular sport anyone could enjoy. Like Peterson, he recognized the need for an easy-to-use field guide and encouraged the young man to produce one.

For several years Peterson taught art during the day and worked on his guide at night. He believed birds could be identified by the size, shape, and color of a few essential features. His simple drawings emphasized the unique characteristics of each species and his text employed clear terms everyone could understand. Arrows on every page pointed out the physical traits bird watchers needed to note.

Finding a publisher was daunting. The United States had just entered the Great Depression. Few editors thought readers would

Roger Tory Peterson, shown in his studio in Old Lyme, Connecticut in this 1993 image, illustrated birds for his popular field guides.

be interested in a book about birds in the middle of the greatest economic crisis the country had ever known. Finally, in 1934, Houghton Mifflin offered to issue 2,000 copies of Peterson's *A Field Guide to the Birds.*

The guide sold out within two weeks. People who couldn't afford fancy vacations discovered they could find adventure in their own backyard or local park. Each weekend, thousands of Americans took to the woods to hunt birds with a book, not a gun.

Peterson revised the guide five times over the next 68 years. In addition, he wrote and illustrated another 50 guidebooks, covering everything from fish to flowers. His fans called him King Penguin, after one of his favorite birds. A new generation of naturalists, dedicated to preserving the environment, drew inspiration from his work. Upon his death in 1996, an editorial in the *New York Times* declared, "He was one of the pioneers in teaching twentieth-century Americans to walk more gently upon their land."

*(continued from page 113)*

society had grown rapidly, enrolling nearly 40,000 members in its first year. Grinnel's articles about the excessive hunting of birds and the destruction of their nests garnered widespread attention. By the late nineteenth century, middle-class Americans had the leisure time to appreciate nature. National pride played a role, too. For the first time, people realized that the natural resources of their country could be as valuable as the artifacts and treasures stored in European museums.

## LEGAL LANDMARKS

Starting in the 1880s, state legislatures began to enact laws forbidding the hunting of scarce species of birds or limiting hunting to certain times of the year. These laws, however, had limited impact. Few merchants cared where their feathers came from. Birds illegally killed in one state could be sold for their plumes in another state without penalty

With the support of the Audubon Society, John Lacey, the U.S. Representative from Iowa, introduced a bill to remedy this situation. His proposed legislation made it a crime to transport protected birds, plants, or animals across state lines. President William McKinley signed the Lacey Act into law on May 25, 1900.

Between 1913 and 1918, the U.S. Congress passed several laws giving national protection to migratory waterfowl. The Migratory Bird Treaty between the United States and Canada in 1918 extended this protection across national borders. It was one of the first international agreements on conservation and served as a model for similar treaties between the Unites States and Mexico in 1934, with Japan in 1972, and with the former Soviet Union (now Russia) in 1976.

## EDUCATING A NEW GENERATION

Educating children about the importance of birds became one of the Audubon Society's first goals. Local chapters distributed bird guides to teachers and invited students to become junior members. The Audubon Society materials emphasized how birds helped farmers by eating insects and distributing seeds. Watching birds sharpened one's powers of observation and developed intellectual skills. In addition, it was quite simply fun.

## KEEPING COUNT

In 1900, Frank Chapman, at that time a curator at the Museum of Natural History in New York, suggested the Audubon Society sponsor an annual Christmas Bird Count. Hunting on Christmas Day had been an old Anglo-American tradition. He wanted people to spend the day counting birds, not killing them. The bird count was open to everyone, young and old. It has continued for more than 110 years and remains one of the society's most popular activities.

In 1998, the Audubon Society started a second annual count, the Great Backyard Bird Count. For four days in February, volunteers keep track of the numbers and kinds of birds that come to a designated area. In 2010, the society received more than 93,600 individual checklists.

These two bird counts help conservation professionals track shifts in the distribution of bird populations over time and document the ways in which birds may be responding to changes in the environment, including climate change.

During the late twentieth century, the Audubon Society became increasingly involved in saving endangered species. In 1966, the U.S. Fish and Wildlife Service released the first list of endangered species in the United States. This paved the way for the Endangered Species Act of 1973, a pioneering piece of legislation that gave the government wide powers to protect the habitats of threatened species on both public and private lands.

On a global level, the International Union for the Conservation of Nature (ICUN) released its own Red List of Threatened Species in 1962. The ICUN worked closely with the World Wildlife Fund, established in 1961, to identify those animals and plants most in need of international protection. In 1963, the two organizations collaborated on the formation of the Convention on International Trade in Endangered Species (CITES), which seeks to promote international agreements on the export of rare plants and animals outside of their natural habitats.

As of 2010, CITES had special programs for the protection of elephants, great apes, falcons, turtles, and rhinoceroses. In March 2010, the convention assembled in the nation of Qatar for a special conference on tigers. "Although the tiger has been prized throughout

## SAVING THE MISSISSIPPI SANDHILL CRANE

New Orleans has found many ways to honor its most important naturalist. The city's greater metropolitan area encompasses no fewer than nine separate museums and parks all bearing the Audubon name. In 1989, these facilities joined together to create the Audubon Nature Institute, one of the country's leading environmental education organizations. The most recent addition to the institute, the Audubon Center for Research in Endangered Species, opened in 1996. One of the center's first projects was saving the Mississippi sandhill crane.

By the 1970s, the Mississippi sandhill crane had become nearly extinct. No more than 35 of these birds remained in the wild. A few breeding pairs still lived in zoos, but attempts to return cranes bred in captivity to their natural habitat had failed. Baby cranes imprint on their caretakers. The hatchlings therefore thought the people who fed them were their parents. Even after the cranes had become adults, they followed humans and could not bond with wild birds.

history, and is a symbol of incredible importance in many cultures and religions, it is now literally on the verge of extinction," declared CITES Secretary-General Willem Wijnstekers. "This must be the year in which we reverse the trend. If we don't, it will be to our everlasting shame."

Audubon once feared that nature would become nothing but a "worn out field." Thanks to conservationists, that dire prediction has so far failed to come true. Yet the campaign to preserve wildlife and wilderness areas, large and small, remains a pressing issue. "Muster all your spirits and go in search of the unknown,"

They had difficulty mating and when they did produce offspring they lacked the instincts to feed and protect them.

The Audubon Center solved this problem by requiring the volunteers who fed the baby cranes to dress in costumes that mimicked the crane's color patterns. The outfit consisted of a large gray sack with a black face screen and covered the person completely. On their hands the volunteers wore realistic crane puppets shaped like the head of an adult crane with a distinctive red crown patch. The hatchlings focused on the red patch, not the person behind the mask.

In the early 2000s, the center began to introduce these puppet-raised cranes into the small wild flock living in the Mississippi Sandhill Crane Wildlife Refuge in Gautier, Mississippi. Slowly but surely the cranes born in captivity bonded with their wild cousins. Between 2000 and 2009, the flock expanded from fewer than 50 to more than 100 birds. The Mississippi sandhill crane continues to be among North America's most endangered species. Thanks to the efforts of the "human cranes" in New Orleans, however, the wild cranes now have a fighting chance for survival.

Audubon exhorted his readers in his introduction to *Birds of America*.

Wherever that unknown may be—from the tundra of Siberia to the rainforest of Brazil, to one's own backyard—the work of John James Audubon continues.

# Selected Images by John James Audubon

American Crossbill

Blue Jay

Blue-Winged Yellow Warbler

Brewer's Blackbird

Chestnut-Backed Titmouse

Downy Woodpecker

Whooping Crane

Mockingbird

Ruff-Necked Hummingbird

Western Bluebird

Yellow-Bellied Flycatcher

Yellow-Crowned Heron

# How to Get Involved

These organizations provide resources to gain information and get involved in ornithology and conservation issues.

**Cornell Lab of Ornithology**
Cornell University
Attn. Communications
159 Sapsucker Woods Rd.
Ithaca, N.Y. 14850
(607) 254-2473
*http://www.birds.cornell.edu*

**Cornell Lab's Project Feeder Watch**
*http://www.birds.cornell.edu/pfw/index.html*
The Cornell Lab of Ornithology is one of the nation's leading study and research centers for the preservation of birds and wildlife. Every winter hundreds of schools, families, and individuals participate in Project Feeder Watch by counting the different kinds of birds that visit their feeders from November to April. Contact the lab via mail or visit its Web site for a research kit containing instructions, tally sheets, and a resource guide to bird feeding.

**National Audubon Society**
225 Varick St., 7th floor
New York, N.Y. 10014
(212) 979-3000
*http://www.audubon.org*

**National Audubon Society's Adopt-A-Bird Program**
*http://www.adoptabird.org*
The National Audubon Society is dedicated to the study and preservation of wild birds and animals throughout the United States.

**133**

Schools and youth clubs can participate in the Adopt-a-Bird Program to sponsor the care and feeding of an injured wild bird in one of the society's bird shelters. Contact your state or local branch of the Audubon Society via mail or visit the Web site above to find out more.

### The Nature Conservancy
4245 North Fairfax Drive, Suite 100
Arlington, Va. 22203-1606
(800) 628-6860
*http://www.nature.org*
The Nature Conservancy is an international organization dedicated to protecting wetlands and other natural areas. Teens who are interested in a career in conservation can work as interns or volunteer at one of the conservancy's nature reserves. Projects may include restoring native plants, identifying animal species, and giving tours to visitors. Contact your state or local branch of the conservancy to find out what opportunities are available in your area.

### National Wildlife Federation
11100 Wildlife Center Drive
Reston, Va. 20190-5362
(800) 822-9919
*http://www.nwf.org*

### National Wildlife Federation's Garden for Wildlife Program
*http://www.nwf.org/gardenforwildlife/index.cfm?campaignid=*
The National Wildlife Federation is dedicated to protecting wild plants and animals and their habitats. Through the Garden for Wildlife Program, schools and community groups can create certified natural habitats for wildlife in their local area. Contact the federation via mail or visit its Web site for a guide to creating and certifying your wildlife habitat.

**U.S. Fish and Wildlife Service Junior Duck Stamp Program and Contest**

Federal Duck Stamp Office

USFWS Department of the Interior

1849 C St. NW

Washington, D.C. 20240

(202) 208-3100

*http://www.fws.gov/juniorduck*

Every year the U.S. Fish and Wildlife Service (USFWS) sponsors a contest open to all students who wish to submit artwork for the service's annual duck stamp. The winning design is sold by the U.S. Post Office to raise money for conservation education. Contact the USFWS or visit its Web site to find out more about the contest's requirements and how to participate.

# Chronology

**1785**    John James Audubon is born (as Jean Rabin) to French planter Jean Audubon and Jeanne Rabin, a servant, in Les Cayes, Haiti, on April 26.

**1791**    John Audubon, 6, arrives in France to live with his father and stepmother, Anne Moynet Audubon.

**1799**    Audubon, at 14 years old, serves in the French navy for a year but suffers from seasickness and decides naval life is not for him.

**1803**    John James Audubon arrives in the United States to oversee a parcel of land his father had purchased in Mill Grove, Pennsylvania.

**1804**    Audubon meets his future wife, Lucy Bakewell, and also begins his first drawings of American birds.

**1805**    Audubon returns to France to ask his father's permission to marry Lucy.

**1806**    Audubon returns to the United States and applies for citizenship.

**1808–1818**    Audubon and Lucy Bakewell marry and move to Kentucky, living first in Louisville and later in Henderson.

**1819**    Audubon begins his career as a professional artist, drawing portraits for money and drawing birds in his spare time.

**1820**    Audubon becomes the artist and taxidermist for the Western Museum of Cincinnati, Ohio; he also goes to New Orleans, where he begins his drawings for *Birds of America*.

**1826–1829**   Audubon travels to England to find an engraver for *Birds of America.*

**1830**   Audubon is elected a member of the Royal Society of London and begins writing his *Ornithological Biography.*

**1831–1833**   Audubon returns to the United States and travels widely, drawing birds and wildlife in South Carolina, East Florida, the Florida Keys, the Gulf of St. Lawrence, and the coast of Labrador.

**1836**   Audubon and his son John Woodhouse are invited to dinner at the White House with President Andrew Jackson.

**1838**   *Birds of America*, a work encompassing four volumes with 435 color drawings of 1,065 birds is finally completed.

**1842**   Audubon buys an estate on Manhattan's Upper West Side; he calls the estate Minnie's Land, after his nickname for his wife, Lucy.

**1843**   Audubon travels along the Upper Missouri River and begins writing his *Missouri River Journals.*

**1846**   Audubon's drawings of mammals, *Viviparous Quadrupeds of North America*, begins publication.

**1851**   Audubon dies at his home, Minnie's Land, on January 27 and is buried in Trinity Cemetery, Manhattan.

**LEGACY**

**1886**   George Grinnell founds the Audubon Society in New York.

**1900**   Naturalist Frank Chapman starts the first annual Christmas Bird Count.

**1901**      U.S. Congress passes the Lacey Act, which protects water birds from being hunted for their plumes.

**1905**      The National Association of Audubon Societies is founded in New York to promote the protection and study of American birds and wildlife.

**1913–1918** U.S. Congress passes several laws protecting migratory birds.

**1923–1924** Audubon society opens its first two wildlife sanctuaries: the Theodore Roosevelt Sanctuary on Long Island, New York, and the Rainey Sanctuary in Louisiana.

**1966**      U.S. Fish and Wildlife Service publishes the first list of endangered species.

**1973**      Congress passes the first Endangered Species Act.

**1985**      U.S. Post Office releases stamps of Audubon's bird paintings to commemorate the bicentennial anniversary of his birth.

**2003**      The Audubon Society of Pennsylvania opens the John James Audubon Center at Audubon's first American home in Mill Grove, Pennsylvania.

# Glossary

**anatomy**   The study of the structure of living organisms, especially animals

**binomial**   A name with two parts; the use of genus and species to identify an organism is an example of binomial classification.

**bird banding**   Marking a bird with an identifying band or tag in order to track its migration patterns and other habits

**botany**   The scientific study of plants

**etching**   A method of producing artwork by carving a drawing onto a metal plate with acid, filling the lines with ink, and pressing a thick piece of paper to the plate to absorb the ink

**Enlightenment** (also French Enlightenment)   An intellectual movement in Europe from about 1750 to 1820 that encouraged the study of science and the use of reason to explain nature and natural phenomena

**extinction**   The elimination of an entire species or subspecies of plants or animals

**folio**   A book made of unbound sheets of paper numbered on both sides, usually secured with ties or buckles to keep the sheets together

**genus**   A biological term for a group of organisms with common characteristics; it is below the category *family* and above *species* in biological taxonomy and is usually indicated by a capitalized Latin name.

**habitat**   The natural environment of a living organism

**hierarchy**   A system that ranks items in order of importance or size

**ichthyology**   The scientific study of fish

**lithography**   A method of reproducing artwork by covering a limestone surface with wax or grease and then engraving a drawing on it to absorb ink for printing; it is generally faster and cheaper than traditional etching.

**migration** (birds)   The seasonal journey made by a species of birds, usually made in response to annual changes in weather conditions

**natural history**   The study of living organisms in their natural environments primarily through observation rather than through experimentation

**nomenclature**   The scientific, academic, or scholarly system of names and formal terms used in a field of study

**ornithology**   The scientific study of birds

**quadruped**   An animal with four feet, usually a mammal

**species**   A group of organisms capable of interbreeding or exchanging genes with one another

**taxidermy**   The practice of stuffing the skins of animals and positioning them in lifelike poses

**taxonomy**   A system of classifying items from large into successively smaller groups; the basic taxonomy of biology is: Life > Domain > Kingdom > Phylum > Class > Order > Family > Genus > Species.

**zoology**   The scientific study of animals

# Bibliography

Audubon, John James. *Audubon and His Journals*. Edited by Maria R. Audubon. New York: Dover Publications, 1986.

———. *Audubon's Birds of America: The Audubon Society Baby Elephant Folio*. New York: Abbeville Press, 2004.

———. *The Audubon Reader*. Edited by Richard Rhodes. New York: Alfred A. Knopf, 2006.

———. *Mississippi River Journal*. New York: Library of America, 1999.

Audubon, John James and John Bachman. *The Quadrupeds of North America*. New York: Arno Press, 1974.

Barrow, Mark V. *Nature's Ghosts: Confronting Extinction from the Age of Jefferson to the Age of Ecology*. Chicago: University of Chicago Press, 2009.

Blunt, Wilfrid. *Linnaeus: The Compleat Naturalist*. Princeton, N.J.: Princeton University Press, 2001.

Darwin, Charles. *The Life of Erasmus Darwin*. Edited by Desmond King-Hele. New York: Cambridge University Press, 2003.

DeLatte, Carolyn E. *Lucy Audubon: A Biography*. Baton Rouge: Louisiana State University Press, 1982.

Ford, Alice. *John James Audubon: A Biography*. New York: Abbeville Press, 1988.

Hill, Geoffrey E. *Ivorybill Hunters: The Search for Proof in a Flooded Wilderness*. New York: Oxford University Press, 2007.

Huxley, Robert, ed. *The Great Naturalists*. London: Thames & Hudson, 2007.

Orr, Oliver H. *Saving American Birds: T. Gilbert Pearson and the Founding of the Audubon Movement*. Gainesville: University of Florida Press, 1992.

Rhodes, Richard. *John James Audubon: The Making of an American*. New York: Alfred A. Knopf, 2004.

# Further Resources

Audubon, John James. *Audubon's Birds of America: The Audubon Society Baby Elephant Folio.* New York: Abbeville Press, 2004.

Brinkley, Edward S. *A Field Guide to the Birds of North America.* New York: Sterling Publishing Co., 2007.

Goodnough, David. *Endangered Animals of North America: A Hot Issue.* Berkeley Heights, N.J.: Enslow Publishers, 2001.

Harrison, Colin James. *Birds of the World.* New York: Dorling Kingsley, 2002.

Hoose, Phillip M. *The Race to Save the Lord God Bird.* New York: Farrar, Straus & Giroux, 2004.

Miles, Victoria. *Wild Science: Amazing Encounters between Animals and the People Who Study Them.* Vancouver: Raincoast Books, 2004.

## WEB SITES

### National Audubon Society: John James Audubon's *Birds of America*

*http://www.audubon.org/bird/BoA/BOA_index.html*

An online exhibit of all the paintings from Audubon's original *Birds of America*, along with an introduction and biography. You can search for birds alphabetically, by state or by their biological family category. There is also a special section highlighting those birds painted by Audubon that are now extinct.

### Pennsylvania Audubon Society: John James Audubon Center at Mill Grove

*http://pa.audubon.org/centers_mill_grove.html*

This site presents a brief biography of Audubon along with links to pages on birds and science. It includes information on the IBA

(Important Bird Area) project, one of the center's programs to help people identify and protect major bird habitats.

**PBS American Masters: John James Audubon: Drawn from Nature**

*http://www.pbs.org/wnet/americanmasters/episodes/john-james-audubon/drawn-from-nature/106/*

An Internet guide to the PBS documentary on John Audubon, with a biography, brief timeline, selection of paintings, and an interview with filmmaker Lawrence Hott.

# Picture Credits

144

# Index

**145**

# About the Author

PATRICE SHERMAN has written both fiction and nonfiction for young readers. She received a bachelor's degree in history from Mount Holyoke College and has worked for many years as an archivist for a variety of libraries and museums. In her spare time, she likes to watch birds at Fresh Pond Reservation, which is only a few blocks from her home in Cambridge, Massachusetts.